CONGRATULATIONS!

Your purchase of
LIFE OF BALANCE vs. IMBALANCE
includes a complimentary offer!

Creating a balanced life does not end with reading a single book. Your response to its contents—creating your individual plan to develop your Balance Triangle, Balance Wheel Core Competencies, and Growth Strategies—will take ongoing, gradual, and incremental effort.

KEEP THE MOMENTUM GOING!

If you are SERIOUS about taking control of the future trajectory of your life, I invite you to call me or visit:

lifeofbalancebook.com
1-888-261-2497

Arrange your complimentary call today regarding coaching and training resources designed to help you on your future personal development journey.

lifeofbalancebook.com
1-888-261-2497

Ed Staub
10 Corral Rd.
Hazleton, Pennsylvania 18202 USA

LIFE OF
BALANCE
vs.
IMBALANCE

8 Paths to Living the Successful
Life You Were Designed For

ED STAUB

Year of the Book
135 Glen Avenue
Glen Rock, PA 17327

ISBN: 978-1-64649-216-9 (paperback)
ISBN: 978-1-64649-230-5 (hardcover)
ISBN: 978-1-64649-217-6 (ebook)

References to all Sandler material used with permission.

Unless otherwise noted, scripture quotations are taken from the *Holy Bible, New Living Translation*, copyright © 1996, 2004, 2007 by Tyndale House Foundation. Used by permission of Tyndale House Publishers, Inc., Carol Stream, IL 60188. All rights reserved.

DEDICATION

To my beloved wife, Tibby, of 51 years.

*I am so thankful for joining me in making God #1
in our lives, which continues to bring
greater meaning into our relationship.*

*I'm eternally grateful for all your love
and for being my best friend on earth!*

CONTENTS

INTRODUCTION

Life is not over until it's over. So until then, it's never too late to change direction. *Life of Balance vs. Imbalance* is for every human being who—regardless of age, sex, shape, color of skin, or ethnicity... and despite current background and life experience—is ready to respond to the challenges of life they are now facing and willing to look in the mirror and commit to taking control.

Yesterday was over at midnight
and there is nothing
you or I can do about it.

It's history. The only real option for a brighter tomorrow and hope-filled future is to begin each new day by looking forward with commitment to learning from past failures, rather than gazing backward, reliving guilt, regrets, and attitudes of being a victim, thus disqualifying ourselves from a potential life of future hope, joy, and success.

This book offers you the ability to conduct your own personal gap analysis of every aspect of your life, along with the tools to change the way you think and act, beginning with the top question you need to answer for the remainder of your time here on Earth:

Who is in control of your life's Balance Wheel?

The answer you choose will determine your exclusive ability to move from a life of unbalance—mistakenly believing you are in control—to a life of balance and purpose, one your creator, God, designed for you.

I am writing days after the problematic withdrawal of U.S. troops from Afghanistan, amidst the COVID-19 pandemic which killed more than six million people, during a period of high inflation, high energy costs, and a manmade open-border crisis created with the intent to change future voting dynamics in the United States forever. There is plenty of imbalance in the world today. Will you be a force for positive change in the world?

Prior to outlining what a balanced journey looks like, I need to confess that I nearly scrapped this book project because of how crazy our world has become. Then I found myself re-reading *Wisdom Walks,* by Dan Britton and Jimmy Page. Their words convinced me of the need for this current volume, one that will help you pursue a differentiated life of balance and excellence rather than one of imbalance and mediocrity.

This thinking will resonate with those I call the "10-percenters"... those whose actions and success rise above 90% of others.

It's all too easy to gravitate toward *shut-down mode* when life gets crazy. But life never slows down. It only gets more hectic and complicated every day. In the midst of this busyness, we lose our ability to live purposefully. It's like we are constantly playing defense, reacting to life instead of creating meaning in it. So instead of doing something, we unplug, sitting on the sidelines to watch life happen.

Disengaging isn't the answer. Not for us, and not for those counting on us. Guess who the next generation is looking to for wisdom? You and me! We can play a significant role in their lives, helping them become all that God wants them to be. We can pass on to them a game plan that prepares them for the challenges and opportunities, and reveals to them God's truth in a relevant, practical way.

You need strategies for dealing with stressful times, recognizing that everything in life is constantly changing. Some changes we like; others we don't. Sometimes the changes are so rapid and relentless, it leaves us reeling, making us feel unable to continue.

Rick Warren, author of *The Purpose Driven Life,* offers these five things to remember when your life changes:

1. Change is unavoidable.

2. Change is not always good, but God uses it for good.

3. God's purpose in every circumstance is to make you more like Jesus.

4. God can even use human error and sin.

5. Every change is always a test of your faith.

He also provides five things to do when you are stressed and overwhelmed:

1. Invest more time alone with God.

2. Ask God to help you see his perspective.

3. Ask God, "What do you want me to learn?"

4. Focus on what never changes.

5. Keep telling God, "I trust you no matter what."

Life of Balance vs. Imbalance is designed to help you answer life's most important question, and resolve to heal the imbalance using the Balance Wheel, a tool to diagnose the eight areas of your life: family, career, mental, physical, emotional, social, spiritual, and financial.

Figure 0-1: The Balance Wheel

Each chapter provides you with the ability to perform a gap analysis between your weaknesses and strengths.

Life of Balance is not another I-centered quick-fix recipe for success, but rather a serious look into the mirror of your life, along with a transferable and reliable plan.

Admit—Commit—Submit

- Admit—Be willing to make life adjustments only you can make as you admit to your messes and failures.

- Commit—Be willing to commit to whatever it takes to learn from those past failures.

- Submit—Be willing to submit to your creator and others to help you finish your life race well.

As your life coach for this journey, it is my privilege to help you discover that you are 100% responsible for your own future. You will now have the tools you need to create a better life for yourself and your family.

Woven throughout your balanced journey is God's promise, found in Jeremiah 29:11: "For I know the plans I have for you," says the Lord. "They are plans for good and not for disaster, to give you a future and a hope."

For all who accept the Life of Balance challenge and are ready to accept God's plan of hope, it's time to begin Day #1 of your future lifeline.

1 | A LIFE OF BALANCE VS. IMBALANCE

Who is in control?

It is time to begin your journey, discovering the who, what, when, where, why, and how of your balanced life. In this chapter I will explain the two wheels—the Balance Wheel, and the Imbalance Wheel.

The major difference between a balanced and imbalanced life stems from your decision about who will be in control of every area of your life. Will you determine to run your life the way you think best, or will you surrender that direction to the creator of the universe who has a perfect plan and purpose for you?

During church services over the years, I have been reminded that our children come to us as gifts from the creator God. A true and sustained life of balance has God's son, Jesus Christ, at the center of the wheel, driving home the need for every spiritual, mental, physical, personal, family, social, career, and financial consideration in life to be directed *by* the creator, versus *upon* the creation.

The goal I set for you is to place your complete trust in the only perfect person who has ever lived—the one who sacrificed everything by being born for the sole purpose of expressing love for the entire world. He has a plan for you to live a life of balance, and ultimately to live a perfect life with him for all eternity.

John 3:16 says: "For this is how God loved the world: He gave his one and only Son, so that everyone who believes in him will not perish but have eternal life."

Figure 1-1: A balanced life with Christ at the center, versus an imbalanced life guided only by I-centered thinking.

In contrast to the Balance Wheel on the left in Figure 1-1 above, notice that the Unbalance Wheel on the right has huge disparities between the quality of life across all eight areas when we try to operate under the belief that we are really the ones in control.

Chapters 4 through 11 will break down the cogs of the Balance Wheel into its respective components, helping you to discover the keys to living a life of balance.

I challenge you to look in the mirror and take personal responsibility for your life... because only 10% of the population does this. But beware, you will no longer be able to look out the window and affix blame on everyone else for the mess in your life. That's what the other 90% does. I'm challenging you to become a "10-percenter."

Throughout the many years of my coaching and business training career, thousands have defined insanity as "doing the same thing over and over again, but expecting a different outcome." However, repeating an action is not, in and of itself, insane… as long as what you are doing is working! The insane part is believing that somehow by duplicating the same ineffective efforts you might be able to produce a new and improved result.

"You can't talk yourself out of a problem that you behaved yourself into." —Stephen Covey

---

Winners behave themselves into a good attitude, instead of waiting to feel good before taking responsibility to do what they don't feel like doing. If you have a good day, it's your fault. And if you have a bad day, it's your fault as well. You see, at the end of each day, the 10% understands that no one owes them anything. They can truly expect a life of balance. But it is up to the individual to replace ineffective behaviors with new and improved behaviors that have worked for other winners since creation began. This is the challenge I now pose to you for each area of your life.

We have been designed to help each other pursue a life of improved and sustained balance. No one can make us do anything. It is up to you to decide who can be trusted as the center of your life.

The business world is often focused on ROI… a return on investment, but in this book we focus instead on achieving ROE… a return on energy. The reason 90% of people achieve only low ROEs in life is because they spend all their time wanting what the 10% have… but they are unwilling to pay the price. They neglect to make an investment of time, energy, and effort to develop a core mindset about the behaviors, attitudes, knowledge, skill sets, and habits that winners exhibit over an extended period of time. That is what allows the 10% to achieve high-level results in every area of life.

The 10% is both willing and able to invest for ROE, day in and day out.

Created in collaboration among Sandler franchises, the AKASH principle explains the sequence of developing those characteristics required of all who lead to greater improvement and lasting results that replenish energy which helps you operate daily on a consistently high level.

| AKASH Acrostic |

A Awareness

K Knowledge

A Application

S Skills Development

H Habit Formation

It takes time to develop good habits. Although God could instantly transform you, he has chosen to develop you slowly. This is how we see him work throughout the Bible. God allowed the Israelites to take over the Promised Land "little by little" so they wouldn't be overwhelmed.[1] Jesus was

---

[1] Deuteronomy 7:22.

deliberate in developing his disciples. In the same way, God prefers to work in incremental steps in your life.

"So get rid of your old self, which made you live as you used to—the old self that was being destroyed by its deceitful desires. Your hearts and minds must be made completely new, and you must put on the new self, which is created in God's likeness and reveals itself in the true life that is upright and holy."[2]

Why does it take so long to change and grow? There are several reasons:[3]

1. We are slow learners

People often have to relearn a lesson 40-50 times to really get it. The problems keep recurring, and we think, "Not again. I've already learned that!" But God knows better. The history of Israel illustrates how quickly we forget the lessons God teaches us and how soon we revert to our old patterns of behavior. We need repeated exposure.

2. We have a lot to unlearn

Since most of our problems—and all of our bad habits—didn't develop overnight, it's unrealistic to expect them to go away immediately. There is no pill, prayer, or principle that will instantly undo the damage of many years. It requires the hard work of removal and replacement. The Bible calls it "taking off the old self" and "putting on the new self."[4]

3. Growth is often painful and scary

There is no growth without change, no change without fear or loss, and no loss without pain. Every change involves a

---

2 Ephesians 4:22-24, *GNT*.
3 https://pastorrick.com/god-grows-you-one-step-at-a-time/
4 Romans 13:12; Ephesians 4:22-24; Colossians 3:7-10, 14.

loss and pain of some kind. People fear these losses. Even if our old ways were self-defeating, they were at least comfortable and familiar, like a worn-out pair of shoes.

4. Good habits take time to develop

Your character is the sum total of your habits. You can't claim to be kind unless you are habitually kind. Your habits define your character. There is only one way to develop the habits of Christlike character. You must practice them. And that takes time! There are no instant habits.

> *Paul urged Timothy, "Practice these things. Devote your life to them so that everyone can see your progress." —I Timothy 4:15, GW*

This process of change develops in stages. First is an awareness of something you desire or are told to achieve by someone else, like a spouse, parent, boss, or friend. Second comes the effort to learn more about the object or subject matter.

Arriving at this point is where half of all people stop. They are unwilling to expend the energy to put the knowledge into practice. About 30% of these people push back, believing their old way of doing things is better. They quit the process without ever reaping the rewards. I call this the "doom loop," because they will need to start the entire process over from the beginning. *Can you hear the insanity siren blaring?*

The third stage is applying the knowledge gained in the first two stages, followed by the fourth stage of skill development, where those who are destined to become winners spend the appropriate time, energy, and effort to hone the new skills.

Now we have reached the place where 10% of the remaining 20% are pleased with their performance and achievement. They begin to scale back their skill development. But the "10-percenters" move to the fifth and final stage of habit formation. This is the ownership phase, where the 10% winners end up achieving their dreams and goals, while the other 90%—who had the same opportunity—now waste what remaining energy they have by making excuses and whining that life is not fair.

If you're still reading, isn't it time you stop making excuses for where you are in life, and instead make a bold new decision to become all that God intended? It's time to begin living a life of purpose which will lead to balance, satisfaction, achievement, and personal joy.

For those who are willing to admit to not having paid the price in the past—but who are committed to this new and improved journey—it is my privilege and pleasure to provide you with a knowledge about what's holding you back, and the direction and skills to move up the achievement scale from mediocrity to "winner," both as a human being and within each role you pursue.

Please don't imagine this process will be comfortable. The 10% who live a balanced life have always understood that "being comfortable" kills performance, because growth and high performance reside beyond your comfort zone. The reality is that most people shy away from what creates discomfort, even though the discomfort will only be temporary.

My goal is to simplify the process of achieving your life of balance. Please understand, I said *simplify*. I did not say it would be *easy*, because if it were easy, everyone would be doing it.

Getting out of your own way is the toughest thing you will ever do in life. You have to break past your comfort zones. Yet if you are finally fed up with living a life of imbalance and mediocrity, and want to give yourself and others in your circle of influence something to shoot for (versus something to shoot at), then I encourage you to consider the following essential self-care factors as a starting point.

Use your answers to help pinpoint the areas where you need the most work.

Questions for Essential Self-Care

1. Am I living the life God intends for me?

2. Do I have a clear, compelling vision for my future?

3. Am I investing time alone each day with God?

4. Does anyone in my life hold me accountable to my best self?

5. Do I consistently make health producing food and drink choices?

6. Am I exercising in some way almost every day?

7. Am I getting sufficient sleep most nights?

8. Do I have at least three close personal relationships?

9. Do I have extra time or margin built into my lifestyle?

10. Am I focused on progress rather than perfection?

The "10-percenters" also realize they don't have to go it alone. They invite extra members to their team who encourage and help them organize and execute their personal development plans.

> *You can't wish yourself out of something*
> *you behaved yourself into.*

Let this be the moment when you decide to replace ineffective and destructive behaviors with effective and positive ones that will lead you to a future of hope, peace, joy, and high performance. This outcome is available to everyone, regardless of your past. The 10% understands that yesterday was over at midnight, and there is nothing they can do about it other than learn from their mistakes and move on.

It's time to let go of all the head trash holding you back. Instead, focus on your future goals and possibilities. Feelings of guilt or playing the victim will only keep you stuck in the past. As Rick Warren reminds, "We are products of our past, but we don't have to be prisoners of it." Let's make this your time for a jail break!

2 | A Life of Balance vs. Imbalance

In the previous chapter, we introduced the concepts of the Balance Wheel and Imbalance Wheel, primarily focusing on the issue of who is at the center and in control of each aspect of your life—God versus you.

The visual wheel brings this into focus, but next let's view the Balance Triangle to understand why a true and sustained life of balance keeps Jesus Christ at its center.

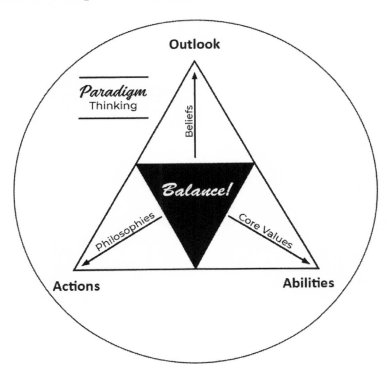

Figure 2-1: How does your Balance Triangle support your Balance Wheel?

This paradigm drives home the need for every spiritual, mental, physical, personal, family, social, career, and financial consideration in life to be directed by our creator, versus living a stress-filled, unhappy, and unfulfilled life, falsely thinking we are in control of our outcomes.

Determining your current levels for each area of the Balance Wheel will help you spotlight key areas for improvement and development. The first step is admitting to a gap between where you are and where you want to be. Consider how you would shade the eight areas on your wheel below:

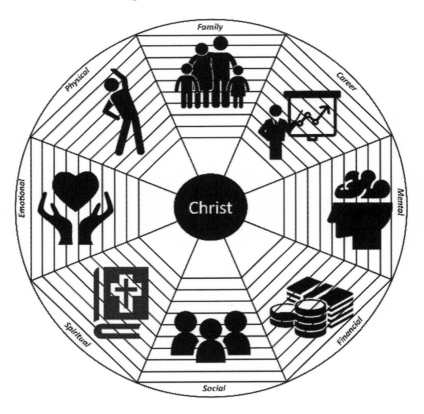

Figure 2-2: Balance Wheel with Christ at the center.

Figure 2-3: Imbalance Wheel where various quadrants are lopsided.

Note that other "Wheel of Life" assessments on the market focus on self versus others. They are predominantly devised as an intellectual process for personal development and pleasure. They were not designed to address the unpopular position that a truly balanced life begins with the most important eternal decision anyone needs to make.

I unashamedly remind you that the creator, God of the universe, claims that central role, but he gives every human being the freedom of choice. Sadly, many choose to hold onto that impossible role, as shown in the Imbalance Wheel (Fig. 2-3) and what a life of imbalance looks and feels like.

It is my desire to help you discover the vast amounts of wasted time, effort, money, resources, and failed relationships that result from a failure to understand and denial of "the truth that sets you free" that's found in the Bible. Jeremiah 29:11 states: "For I know the plans I have for you," says the Lord. "They are plans for good and not for disaster, to give you a future and a hope."

Would you like to know what those plans are for you, and how to access this tremendous hope both for your present life and your eternal future? This endeavor is not some prosperity name-it-and-claim-it message, offering only false hope and disappointment to make political and spiritual heroes richer and more powerful while the masses suffer.

Subsequent chapters will focus on each specific spoke of the Balance Wheel, understanding your life as it is now, while offering proven truths, attitudes, behaviors, and skills that the "10-percenters" have used to become highly effective individuals since the beginning of time.

Car Analogy

Is your life's "drive" smooth or bumpy? As we continue through this journey, you will be constantly challenged to look into the mirror and assess each area of your life. Although separate, there are no standalone categories. Each life role impacts others simultaneously.

For example, your physical health impacts your mental capacity, social, family, and career areas. To help you understand the importance of achieving a greater ROE—return on energy—consider the following automobile exercise as you evaluate whether your Life Wheel is balanced or imbalanced.

Select a high-end automobile that is known for having a smooth ride. Many people think of Mercedes, Lexus, or BMW. Once you acknowledge that this brand new automobile has four perfectly balanced wheels prior to leaving the car dealership, I then ask you to replace just one of those balanced wheels with an imbalanced one. Now take your car for a test drive. Evaluate the ride. Did you change your prediction from a smooth ride to a bumpy one?

Notice how quickly your attitude shifted about the new purchase, even considering the substantial investment made. Also remember that even high-end automobiles eventually break down and need to be replaced. For many people, that's between 5-20 times across a lifespan, at phenomenal cost of time, effort, and money.

The creator of the universe only gave us one machine (our body) to inhabit during this entire lifespan. For the most part, it is left to us and our choices regarding the time, effort, and money invested that determines how balanced and smoothly it runs. Remember, just like manufacturers of high-end automobiles—who design their cars to run smoothly on a multitude of road surfaces—our God of the universe created and designed each of us to trust in him for a smooth ride on all of our bumpy and chaotic road conditions of life.

And just like the high-end automobile manufacturers would not honor a warranty if the vehicle was misused, the creator of our bodies will not be responsible for the imbalanced lives we live as a result of choices to misuse our bodies as they were designed to operate.

The Choice Is Yours!

Just like a high-end automobile travels on roads to many kinds of destinations, our human journey is on the Road to Authenticity—the journey to becoming authentic and balanced, both to ourselves and others within our sphere of influence. This Road to Authenticity is only made possible by traveling through the walls of vulnerability and accountability on either side of this exclusive highway.

The process of change is made up of three sequential elements: Admit, Commit, Submit. The challenge for your journey toward the destination of a balanced, happy, effective, and fulfilling life is point one.

Admit—Commit—Submit

- Who will you *admit* to needing help from on your journey?

- What attitudes, behaviors, knowledge, and skills do you *commit* to acquiring and honing to achieve your Balance Wheel improvement goals?

- Who will you *submit* to holding you accountable along your journey?

Closing Point

Change is not the ultimate goal, but rather improvement. The process is ongoing, gradual, and incremental. It is not a quick-fix program. Only the right behaviors performed consistently over time lead to effective results.

"Everything you do in life matters!"
—*Andy Andrews*

---

3 | WHY CHANGE?

A better way to live

During this part of the journey, we discuss why we should change, while providing a roadmap, useful tools, and a plan to follow toward living a life of balance.

So often we discover that we are working on the wrong end of the problem. There is a difference between Effectiveness and Efficiency.

While the 90% are driven toward efficiency—doing *lots* of things right and using *lots* of technology and hoping for quick-fix results—the 10% of highly successful people are instead driven toward effectiveness by being laser focused on doing the *right* things right. That 10% also use technology, but primarily to help drive their long-term Hedgehog Concept (Fig. 3-1) as described by Jim Collins in *Good to Great*.

Figure 3-1: The Hedgehog Concept

The Hedgehog Concept helps us understand the connection or congruency of our thoughts—meaning how we think (our paradigms), our life beliefs, philosophies, concepts, and principles that determine our core values. These are then manifested and proven through moment by

17

moment, daily application of our attitudes, behaviors, skills, and knowledge.

The Hedgehog Concept uses three intersecting circles, emphasizing what you, your family, and your organizations want to be known for, whether it be a personal or professional brand. All three circles intersect at the center where a BHAG—big, hairy, audacious goal—becomes possible.

The left circle asks what you have decided to strive to become best at in the world. The top circle involves your passion for making the first circle a reality. The right circle is about what drives your economic engine, achieving the greatest ROI for your time, energy, and money to make your Hedgehog Concept an ongoing reality.

Consider your answers to these Hedgehog questions and select a BHAG that represents your "Why" in life. What drives you to invest everything it takes to achieve the type of life and results you have determined to be important, regardless of what anyone else thinks about your plan for a fulfilling and balanced life?

At some point, when the pain of failing is great enough, we eventually learn that we have been working on the wrong end of the problem. Ultimately, there are only two ways to learn. First, through experiences, learning from our own mistakes, and second, through wisdom, learning from the mistakes of others.

The Balance Triangle (Fig. 3-2) is designed to help us adjust or correct our paradigms, our way of thinking, based on core values, beliefs, and philosophies that drive the success of the 10%. Employing those outlook, actions, and abilities are what result in a pathways to success.

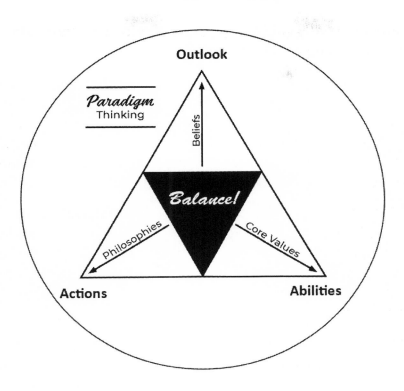

Figure 3-2: Balance Triangle.

My desire is to help you discover the same path to success that is proven, reliable, repeatable, and transferable—regardless of your sex, shape, age, ethnicity, background, or pedigree. The change you desire is possible! You don't have to be a victim or prisoner of the past for the Balance Triangle and other tools to work. The key is discovering where your past thinking, beliefs, behaviors, attitudes, and skills were either improperly used, or not used at all.

As we break down each area of the Balance Triangle, I trust you will *admit* to the existence of gaps, *commit* to developing a total model of success, and *submit* to others who have a proven track record of successful, balanced lives.

This triangle reflects the way you believe, think, feel, and act throughout your day to day life. Inside the triangle, reference points of success determine your "Why," the non-negotiable core values you decide to live by. Your paradigms, or ways of thinking, are represented by the circle surrounding your triangle, which influence how you behave. The world teaches you to think primarily the way the majority thinks, but God tells us that as a man or woman thinks, that is how they will behave or act.[5]

Your outlook to the world of 90% tells you that it should be driven by good thoughts and motivational one-liners, which will fuel your actions... "just do it" and feel good about yourself. Reflecting on the 2020 global shutdown, paralyzed by pandemic fears, featuring the highest drug use, depression, and suicide rates in the history of humankind, how is that advice working out? Those same self-proclaimed experts advise us to stay at home in fear, which actually subverts effective behaviors for living.

The 10% focus their outlook on their God-given identity, which tells them that no one is more or less important than anyone else as a human being as we all are made in God's perfect image. We will greatly expand on this point throughout our spiritual, emotional, and personal chapters.

The 10% also expand their outlook by checking on their identity, their career and work, and their abundance versus scarcity mentality regarding potential levels of success.

Actions—It's What We Do

Where the 90% only undertake a beneficial action if they feel like it, the 10% do the right things right, regardless of how they feel. The 10% achieve more success and balanced lives because they know that the only thing they can control are their actions, not the results. They take responsibility for

---

[5] Proverbs 23:7 (NKJV)

their lives and proactively behave themselves into a good outlook, while the 90% opt for feeling disenfranchised, making excuses, and affixing blame outside of themselves rather than doing or changing something to improve their situation.

The motto of the 90% is that "knowledge is power." They believe it determines who and how much success one should be allowed to have. In contrast, the 10% develops and refines awareness and knowledge through application of skills and the formation of success habits. Their motto is "properly applied knowledge is power." This is where effectiveness versus efficiency really differentiates!

Admit—Commit—Submit

- As you reflect on the Hedgehog Concept and Balance Triangle, ask yourself what you are willing to *admit* that either has you on the wrong track entirely or is holding you back.

- What new outlooks, actions, and abilities do you *commit* to acquiring and implementing to achieve your Balance Wheel improvement goals?

- Who will you be vulnerable to *submit* to holding you accountable along your journey toward authenticity and a life of balance?

Closing Point

All the winners at life decide what they want to be best in the world at. They are passionate about what they do and become in life. They behave regardless of how they feel.

Winners understand that improvement is an inside/outside process. They take 100% responsibility for their lives... no excuse making. Their motto is, "If I have a good day, it's my fault. And if I have a bad day, it's my fault."[6] The response is everything!

---

[6] Paul G, Stultz, Ph.D., *Adversity Quotient*.

4 | MENTAL

Rethinking your life

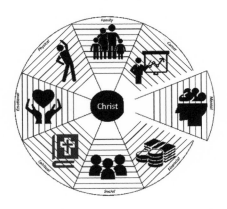

Now that we have discussed how to begin to use tools to recognize your blind spots and life areas to improve, the next eight chapters will deal with analyzing the eight respective areas of your Balance Wheel.

It is important to remember that each life area directly impacts other areas. For example, your physical well-being affects not only the mental, emotional, and social aspects of your life, but also your career capabilities. As we dissect specific areas in each chapter, we will connect the dots to other affected areas.

Although the primary purpose of *Life of Balance vs. Imbalance* is to encourage you to come to grips with who is in control of your life's Balance Wheel (which we'll dig into more deeply in the spiritual chapter), we begin with the Mental aspect—how to manage your mind for more effective living.

Realize that it is impossible to change your behaviors until you change the way you think! Over the years of my coaching and training business, I have been asked what is my primary goal for helping people. I quickly respond that I am in the "trash removal business." We need to manage our minds for more effective living.

I want to be clear that the focus in the Mental area relates to how a person thinks, rather than how much knowledge one has accumulated. As a lifetime learner who categorizes himself as a "full-time project," I have observed the unwise assertion by some that those possessing high IQ and GPAs are entitled to run the world. They also insist that anyone with less of an intellectual pedigree should step aside and not question their expert status.

From a perspective of global predictors of success, Dr. Thomas Stanley studied how winners think, capturing empirical data on nearly any success point you could imagine. In *The Millionaire Mind,* he shared that those who have achieved deca-millionaire results more often maintain higher levels of balanced lives than those who possess higher IQs.

A glaring paradigm buster that debunks traditional thinking was the belief that highly successful winners would score at genius level, around 1600, on SAT college entrance exams. In reality, the average was in the 1170-1200 range.

Dr. Paul G. Stoltz spent 19 years researching and 10 years applying his data, released in a 1997 bestselling book *Adversity Quotient: Turning Obstacles into Opportunities,* that success in life and work are largely determined by one's Adversity Quotient (AQ).

Your AQ tells you how well you will withstand adversity and be able to surmount it. It predicts who will overcome adversity and who will be crushed by it. It also predicts who will exceed performance expectations and who will fall short. Finally it predicts who will give up and who will prevail.

Stoltz's research goes on to compare not only AQ to IQ, but also EQ—emotional intelligence—as global predictors of success. In the end, a high IQ comes in a distant third when evaluating highly successful and balanced individuals, since the ego of those with high IQ rarely allows them to admit they could be wrong.

That being said, our primary comparison throughout the remainder of our conversation will be God's Word, the Bible, where we present biblical teachings concerning the state of our lives versus the worldview. The book of Proverbs was written by King Solomon, recognized as the wisest and wealthiest person of all time. In the end, this wisest and wealthiest person of all time deemed everything meaning-less, including his own knowledge and wealth. He stopped thinking and trusting in the Lord. You can read about his loss of balance and fall from power in the book of Ecclesiastes which he also wrote in his later years.

The Bible reminds us: "Fix your thoughts on what is true, and honorable, and right, and pure, and lovely, and admirable. Think about things that are excellent and worthy of praise."[7]

Stress Management Starts in the Mind

More people than ever are being negatively impacted by stress, particularly due to an over-the-top response to the COVID-19 pandemic. Yes, the virus is real. It is serious, but the side effects of quarantine and lockdown have merely

---

[7] Philippians 4:8.

created more stress, including an increase in depression and risk for suicide.[8]

The battle with stress in your life is going on between your ears. The battle is in your mind. It's in your thought life. What you fill your mind with determines the level of stress in your life. If you want peace of mind, you're going to have to start controlling what you allow inside your brain. Whatever you put in your mind is going to come out in your life. If you want to lower your stress, you have to change what you think about.

Philippians 4:8 gives us eight tests for whether we should allow something in our mind. Ask yourself:

1. Is it good?
2. Is it worthy of praise?
3. Is it true?
4. Is it honorable?
5. Is it right?
6. Is it pure?
7. Is it beautiful?
8. Is it respected?

The secret conversations you hold in the privacy of your own mind are shaping your destiny little by little. Research indicates that the average person thinks approximately 50,000 thoughts per day. This is either good or bad news, because every thought moves you either toward your God-given potential or away from it. No thoughts are neutral. Whatever you direct your mind to think about will ultimately be revealed for everyone to see.

You need to understand that you have one thing in life over which you have complete control—your thinking. This

---

[8] According to Dr. Elizabeth Reichert of Stanford Psychiatry.
https://med.stanford.edu/psychiatry/about/covid19/anx.html

profoundly influences every other aspect of your life. In my practice as a life coach, I have observed that all lasting change is preceded by changed thinking. Any other type of change will be only temporary. The place to begin then is with your thought life, with a revival of your mind.

I have great news for you. You no longer have to be a slave to your thoughts! Few people have experience with intentional focused thinking. We spend very little time thinking about what we are thinking about. For most of us, thinking is a poorly developed ability that often occurs with little conscious effort.

Managing Your Mind for More Effective Living

Your mental health is a critical part of your effectiveness in living. But it's easy to think that your problems have more to do with your circumstances—a lack of resources or personal struggle you're facing—and less to do with how you think. But the truth is, God is far more interested in changing your mind than your circumstances.

We want God to change our circumstances and take away the pain and sorrow around us. Those issues are important, but God wants to first deal with what's going on inside. The Apostle Paul tells us, "Don't copy the behavior and customs of this world, but let God transform you into a new person by changing the way you think. Then you will learn to know God's will for you, which is good, pleasing and perfect."[9] Nothing will change in your life unless you change how you think!

Why is mental health so important?

Your thoughts control your life. Every single action begins with a thought. If we don't think it, we don't do it. Proverbs

---

[9] Romans 12:2.

4:23 says: "Guard your heart above all else, for it determines the course of your life." Even untrue thoughts will shape your entire life if you don't check them.

The mind is the battleground for sin. We win or lose based on our thoughts. All temptation happens in the mind. Paul describes this battle: "I love God's law with all my heart. But there is another power within me that is at war with my mind. This power makes me a slave to the sin that is still within me."[10]

Your brain is your greatest asset and the devil wants to control it. Managing your mind is the key to peace and happiness. An unmanaged mind leads to tension, pressure, and conflict. A managed mind leads to tranquility, serenity, and confidence. Romans 8:6 advises: "Letting your sinful nature control your mind leads to death. But letting the Spirit control your mind leads to life and peace."

Daily Habits to Cultivate a Healthy Mind

Feed your mind with truth

We all know the importance of nutrition. Good calories help you grow stronger and give you more energy. Bad calories harm your body. The same is true with your thoughts. For a healthy thought life, you need to feed your mind with truth, not poison or junk. Jesus told us about healthy "mind food" when he told Satan, "People do not live by bread alone, but by every word that comes from the mouth of God."[11]

Free your mind from destructive thoughts

Your mind needs to be liberated. You are a prisoner of your thoughts. You've been told all kinds of untrue things about

---

[10] Romans 7:22-23.
[11] Matthew 4:4.

yourself. You believe many of them, and those thoughts control your actions. As Rick Warren suggests, "We are products of our past, but we don't have to be prisoners of it."

Remember that dwelling on your problems doesn't fix them; it just makes you an expert on them. Due to our human nature, we live in a society bent on highlighting what is wrong with just about everything. This is so common that most people hardly notice it anymore. Good news does not make the front page. Our entire 2020 presidential election was stark evidence of this unfortunate reality. When you think a limiting thought without challenging it, your mind buys into it.

To counteract this, remind yourself that negative thoughts do not come from God. God is positive toward everything but sin. If a thought brings about worry, fear, or fatigue, it is not from God. After all, the Bible tells us, "For God has not given us a spirit of fear and timidity, but of power, love and self-discipline."[12] If a thought leads you to feel like a victim instead of a victor, it is not from God. Paul also tells us, "But thank God! He gives us victory over sin and death through our Lord Jesus Christ."[13]

Though we are engineered for success, it is very easy to inadvertently program ourselves for mediocrity if we neglect to think positive, goal-directed thoughts. Productive thinking and destructive thinking are both merely habits. Because your thinking is not fixed, it can constantly be improved when you make a commitment to do so.

Remember, each moment is a new beginning. Your future is not defined by your past. Your thoughts can change, and consequently your future life can become totally different.

---

[12] II Timothy 1:7.
[13] I Corinthians 15:57.

Negative thinking corrupts your brain and triggers harmful mental states such as anxiety, moodiness, depression, and irritability. Unless you train your mind constructively, your thinking becomes automatic, impulsive, and often erroneous. Your thoughts often misrepresent reality by bending, distorting, deleting, exaggerating, or otherwise manipulating the truth (the perfect definition for *Fake News!*).

Paul reminds us that we have a choice. With God's help, we can control our thoughts. Further, his words teach us that the choice is between good and bad, between excellence and mediocrity. Life is never completely good or completely bad. There will always be some junk and there will always be some greatness. Your marriage, your health, and your finances may be in outstanding condition, but you might be facing learning difficulties with one of your children. Maybe your kids are all thriving, but your marriage is in an exasperating rut. Or perhaps your family life is wonderful, but you're disappointed with your circle of friends, your weight, your faith, or the condition of your home.

You will always have something to complain about, and you will always have some blessings to count. Inevitably, life is filled with peaks and valleys, but even in the valleys, there will always be something working really well in your life; and even on the mountain peaks, everything will not be perfect. Life is always a mixture of good and bad.

Whether you choose to count your blessings or to complain, it's helpful to understand that you have a choice. This is true of life as a whole, as well as in all specific areas of your life.

Do you want to break those habits and gain more control over the way you think? Then you need to hear and understand this truth: *You do not have to believe everything you think.*

Your mind lies to you all the time. Just because you think something doesn't make it true. Just because you feel something doesn't make it true. Your mind and your emotions lie to you. Part of spiritual growth is becoming more like Jesus, learning to know the difference between thoughts that are true and false, and those that are not.

Focus on the Right Things

Philippians 4:8 tells us: "Fix your thoughts on what is true, and honorable, and right, and pure, and lovely, and admirable. Think about things that are excellent and worthy of praise." What are the good things we should focus on? Think about Jesus. You've heard the old cliché that you become what you think about the most. If you think about Jesus, you'll become more like him. So when you're ready to give up, think about Jesus.

Next, think about others. Everything in the world teaches you to think about yourself and no one else, but the Bible tells us that life isn't about us. You only know the real meaning of life when you learn to give your life away.

Think about eternity. Life is about more than the here and now. Too often we have short-term thinking. Colossians 3:2 says: "Think about the things of heaven, not the things of earth." You've heard people say of others that they are too heavenly minded to be any earthly good. That's not true. It's the heaven-minded people who have done the most good throughout history.

Learning to manage your mind will change your life and your balance. God gave you your mind and it's one of your greatest assets. It's time to go to battle for it every day.

Change is possible, and you can do all things through Christ, who gives you strength.[14] Even after you become a follower of Jesus, there's a tension inside of you. You have your good nature that God gave you, and you also have your own nature that is pulling at you. But there is a way out.

Jesus promised: "You will know the truth and the truth will set you free."[15] The secret to personal change is not willpower or something you do or say. It's not a pill, resolution, or a vow you make. The secret to personal change is something you know. You know the truth. When you change the way you think, it changes the way you feel. And when you change the way you feel, it changes the way you act.

Behind every self-defeating act is a lie you believe. It may be a lie about yourself, your past or future, God or others. Why do you do something that you know is bad for you? You do it because you think there's some kind of payoff. That's the lie! You can only change and fulfill God's purpose for your life if you start with God's truth. If you want to change the way you live, you need to start, and that needs to begin in your mind.

You need to know and believe God's truth. When you know the truth, the truth will set you free.[16]

How Do You Think?

What do you think it means to know God's truth? Think of the lies that have been playing on repeat in your head for years. Which of God's truths do you need to replace them with? What will it take for you to know God's truth better? What changes do you need to make in your life?

---

[14] Philippians 4:13.
[15] John 8:32.
[16] Supplemental scriptures regarding God's truth as it applies to the mind: Matthew 22:37; Romans 8:5-8; I Corinthians 1:18-29; II Corinthians 4:4; Ephesians 4:20-24; Philippians 3:19; Colossians 3:2

Admit—Commit—Submit

- What worldview thinking are you ready to *admit* to that is negatively impacting your Balance Wheel?

- What biblical view are you ready to *commit* to pursuing to replace negative and ineffective ways of thinking?

- Who are you prepared to *submit* to for regular accountability regarding your new commitments on thinking differently?

Knowledge is not power unless it is properly applied. Knowledge has true value under only three conditions:

- If it involves worthy matters
- If it is held by people of worthy character
- If it is used in a worthy manner

Closing Scripture

"Don't copy the behavior and customs of this world, but let God transform you into a new person by changing the way you think. Then you will learn to know God's will for you, which is good, pleasing and perfect." (Romans 12:2)

Jesus promised: "You will know the truth and that truth will set you free." (John 8:32)

Moving forward into our next area, we will dissect your work life or career path. Will we discover that we are stressed-out workaholics or a fulfilled person living with purpose? Stay tuned to find out.

5 | CAREER

Who controls your work?

Realizing that the average adult spends between 50-75% of waking hours, five or more days a week, either at work or commuting, the career area of your Balance Wheel is next.

On the heels of our discussion regarding the mental area, our challenge continues for you to look in the mirror and admit, commit, and submit to a change of thinking that has historically left you unhappy and unfulfilled in your work or career path.

In the event you love your work and career—and the time and effort involved do not negatively impact the other seven areas of your Balance Wheel—you have my permission to skip this chapter. However, most fall into one of the following groups of workers surveyed:

1. Over 50% of U.S. workers are unhappy in their jobs.[17]

2. Only 27% of college graduates end up working in the field of their major, a significant reason why most are frustrated, stressed, and unfulfilled, especially after broken promises by higher education about a great track record for career placement. Couple that with the fact that so many graduates have spent an average of $100,000-200,000 in tuition—much of which is through loans that need to be paid back with interest—and are ill prepared to handle the brutal facts of their reality.[18]

It is important to consider the benefit of expensive and highly ineffective training, in both the short and long term. Perhaps a non-traditional preparation for a career path is for you. The first significant change in thinking is for parents to stop applying pressure, directly and indirectly from birth, on a blind obsession with grades, and getting into the "right" college. Neither of these guarantee lifelong success, or lack of it, based on income, possessions, and accumulation of things versus happiness, passion, and an overall balanced life.

Since this is at the top of the list of parental blind spots, I trust you will consider an old Zig Ziglar quote: "You need a checkup from the neck up, because you have a case of stinkin' thinkin'." Look into the mirror to shed light on the insanity of your current thinking about career preparation for your kids.

Let's go back to the more than 50% who feel they are unhappy in their jobs. Many in this group claim the primary

---

[17] *Forbes.com*, Oct. 25, 2019.
[18] New York Federal Reserve Bank with *Inside Higher Ed*, database of 125M professional profiles compiled by E.M.S.I.

reason for job dissatisfaction results from companies underpaying workers. Paying bills with limited income causes stress.

In some cases, employees just feel they're underpaid even when they may be receiving a fair wage. This happens because society spends a lot of time and energy comparing us to one another and our lot in life. When we later look at our financial reality and goal-setting behaviors, we will discover that income level is rarely the true reason for job dissatisfaction and stress.

Developing for Career Effectiveness

Regardless of your current reality, whether you are dissatisfied or fearful of the work-life possibilities you face as you prepare for your career, this section is intended to provide you with a better understanding of what it really takes to become successful, balanced, and happy as you pursue or make adjustments to your career path.

Based on my 50+ years of real-world observations and experiences in the fields of sales, management, leadership and human dynamics, and growth and development, I want to challenge worldview thinking that places nearly the entire emphasis on the accumulation of product knowledge—measured by test score, GPA, class ranking, and degrees achieved. I'm not against higher education, but the Theory–Application–Experience (TAE) model of learning offers little firsthand application or experience, and many business owners are disappointed with the overall abilities brought to the marketplace.

Flipping the TAE Model—EAT

Following decades of hiring and paying high wages based on the TAE learning model, only to be disappointed with the level of results received, highly successful businesses have begun to train, coach, and mentor their own employees. They have flipped the TAE learning model completely to become the EAT model—emphasizing real-world *experiences*, resulting from proven *applications*, supported by appropriate *theory*. They direct their recruiting, hiring, and training resources to those applicants and employees who are assessed as "best fit" candidates based on criteria for success that has proven reliable and transferrable across various job positions and business disciplines.

These winning owners and organizations made the transition away from depending solely on high IQ and GPAs to instead seek highly motivated individuals who are trainable, rather than legends in their own minds who already have everything figured out. Instead, they seek to hire individuals who bring the must-haves—character, initiative, motivation, and people skills—knowing they will learn the nice-to-haves while they are already achieving at higher levels in early stages of employment.

In comparison to previous hiring criteria, these highly successful people and organizations have embraced assessments based on:

- Core competencies and corresponding behaviors

- Crucial elements of success—desire, commitment, responsibility, and outlook

- Hidden weaknesses—decision-making process, money weaknesses, need for approval, emotional involvement, and overcoming rejection

- Behavioral analysis—using extended DISC, which stands for (D) Dominant or Drivers, (I) Influencers,

(S) Steady Relations, and (C) Compliant or Cautious Thinkers.

These overall findings determine an individual's hiring quotient for success by identifying their key performance indicators, winners' attributes, and team matrix (how each candidate will or will not work together with other team members).

At the end of the day, these assessments provide pinpointed onboarding opportunities for training new hires and excellent evaluation tools for team members to further develop core competencies and behaviors, while mitigating weaknesses that have yet to be developed.

What has been discovered through the use of these identifiers of strengths and weaknesses is that they represent the same competencies, attitudes, and behaviors needed for success in all areas of Balance Wheel development.

Who Is at the Center?

I trust this exploration has enlightened you on why so many people struggle to succeed and remain unhappy in their work or chosen career path. We conclude this chapter by once again asking the central question. Who is in control of your life and career?

For those who are truly interested in pursuing a fulfilling career path and work life, I'll give you a hint. This person is not you, your parents, guidance counselors, or others, but rather God who created you with the talents and abilities to pursue a life purpose he created for you to live.

The #1 decision everyone needs to make is who they will place at the center of their life wheel. Will it be you or will it be Jesus Christ?

If you want your life to turn from emptiness to overflowing, then give Jesus complete control, including over your career! A biblical example is when Simon Peter let Jesus get into his boat so he could teach people standing on the shore. The Bible says: "When he [Jesus] had finished speaking, he said to Simon Peter, 'Put out into the deep water and let down the nets for a catch.' Simon answered, 'Master, we've worked hard all night and haven't caught anything. But because you say so, I will let down the nets'."[19]

Then the story continues in the next two verses to say after they had done so, they caught such a large number of fish that their nets began to break. So they signaled their partners in another boat to come and help them, and they came and filled both boats so full that they began to sink.

If you want your life to turn from emptiness to overflowing, you've got to get Jesus in your boat. But what's your "boat"? It's how you make a living. Simon's business was his boat because he was a fisherman. The "boat" represents your career, your profession, your job, just like it represented Simon Peter's entire livelihood.

What does it mean to have Jesus in your boat? It means you dedicate your career to God. I'm not talking about salvation here. You may have Jesus in your life, but have you given him control of your career? You may have served faithfully in church, but when you go back to work during the week, is Jesus the one you trust at your job or do you put Jesus on the shelf?

When Simon Peter gave his job over to Jesus, he was in turn blessed with incredible results. But don't miss the sequence. We sometimes think, *"God, make me really successful in business and then I'll serve you with the success."* Wrong!

[19] Luke 5:4-5 (NIV).

It's the exact opposite. Peter first gave Jesus control of his job, then Jesus blessed Peter's job with enormous success. That's the proper order. "Seek the kingdom of God above all else, and live righteously, and he will give you everything you need."[20]

Notice the emphasis on need versus want. When you want God to bless something, put him first in that area. You want God to bless your time? Give him the first part of your day every day. You want God to bless your money? Give him the first 10% of your income... no matter how small it is. You want God to bless your job? Give him control, no matter how successful you are.

God's desire for everyone can be found in Ecclesiastes 5:19, where it says: "And it is a good thing to receive wealth from God and the good health to enjoy it. To enjoy your work and accept your lot in life—this is indeed a gift from God." So whether you are well along in your work life or just starting out, you need to get Jesus in your boat and you'll see your life turn from empty to overflowing.

Questions to Consider:

- What would it look like if you gave control of your job to Jesus?

- What are your fears or concerns about making God the center of your career?

- How do you want God to bless you in your career?

- What do you think he wants you to do first?

---

[20] Matthew 6:33.

Admit—Commit—Submit

What worldview thinking are you ready to *admit* to that is negatively impacting your thinking regarding your career or work life?

What biblical view are you ready to *commit* to pursuing to replace negative and ineffective ways of thinking and approaching your work life and career path?

Who are you prepared to *submit* to for regular accountability regarding your new commitments on thinking differently about your work life and career path?

Closing Scripture

"Do not work for food that spoils, but for food that endures to eternal life, which the son of man [Jesus] will give you." (John 6:27, *NIV*)

"But on the judgment day, fire will reveal what kind of work each builder has done. The fire will show if a person's work has any value." (I Corinthians 3:13)

"We work wearily with our own hands to earn our living." (I Corinthians 4:12)

"Work willingly at whatever you do, as though you were working for the Lord rather than for people." (Colossians 3:23)

"Make it your goal to live a quiet life, minding your own business and working with your hands, just as we instructed you before. Then people who are not believers will respect the way you live, and you will not need to depend on others." (I Thessalonians 4:11-12)

"Even while we were with you, we gave you this command: 'Those unwilling to work will not get to eat'."
(II Thessalonians 3:10)

Final Thought

Find what you are good at, and do it. Evaluate your gifts and abilities. Pursue the career God equipped you for. Resist the temptation to take a job based on convenience or pressure from friends. Discover what motivates and excites you. Then pour yourself into something you can believe in.

"To rejoice in his labor;
this is the gift of God."
—Ecclesiastes 5:19, KJV

6 | EMOTIONAL

Developing your emotional life

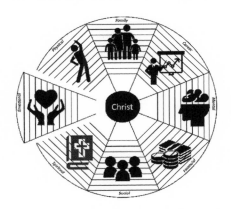

Jesus said: "Come to me, all of you who are weary and carry heavy burdens, and I will give you rest."[21] Are you weary of life and feeling emotionally drained, dealing with life's constant challenges and chaos?

If you answered yes, let's look at how emotions impact other areas of life, and indeed how every decision we make will benefit from increased emotional strength.

II Corinthians 4:17 says: "For our present troubles are small and won't last very long. Yet they produce for us a glory that vastly outweighs them and will last forever!"

A Sandler principle that has benefited me greatly over the past three decades as to how to deal with trials and troubles states: "When you get emotionally involved (the wrong, hurtful way) in any issue or situation, you get killed!" This is

---

21 Matthew 11:28.

a slow and painful sort of death because the 90% struggles mightily with emotional imbalance and has a strong tendency to view most everything from a glass-half-empty, short-term perspective, which results in negative, hurtful, emotional responses.

Which Wolf Will You Feed?

Let's expand your awareness of this unfortunate and self-defeating reality, and offer helpful alternatives for how you can think about and respond to negative emotions once you take responsibility for your own emotional life.

Identifying Productive/Helpful
and Unproductive/Hurtful Emotions

The following classic fable asks you to choose your future responses.

> A grandfather tells his grandchild about two wolves battling inside his heart. "One is wise and kind and the other is vicious and cruel," says the grandfather.
>
> "Which one will win?" asks the grandchild.
>
> The grandfather replies, "The one I feed."

Which one will you choose to feed? The hurtful joy steelers and emotional drainers? Or the healthy and positive emotional energy producers?

As you review the following list, identify the dominant emotions which drive your life.

Unproductive/Hurtful Emotions:

- *Bitterness* shows you where you need to heal, where you're still holding judgments toward others and yourself.

- *Resentment* shows you that you're living in the past and not allowing the present to be as it is.

- *Discomfort* shows you that you need to pay attention right now to what is happening because you're being given the opportunity to change, to do something different than how you typically do it.

- *Anger* shows you what you're passionate about, where your boundaries are, and what you believe needs to change about the world.

- *Disappointment* shows you that you tried for something, that you did not give in to apathy, that you still care.

- *Guilt* helps you understand the person that you do not want to be. It gives you the opportunity to forgive yourself in order to move on.

- *Shame* shows you that you're internalizing other people's beliefs about who you should be, or who you are, and that you need to reconnect with yourself.

- *Sadness* shows you the depth of your feeling, the depth of your care for others in this world.

Productive/Helpful Emotions:

- *Forgiveness* extends grace to others, knowing that you have been forgiven.

- *Passion* lets you focus intensely on your life, purpose, and goals while striving to be the best you can be.

- *Gratefulness* allows you to recognize the love of God in everything he has given us, and to know that he has given us everything.

- *Agape love* is a love that is willingly extended to others, whether they deserve it or not.

- *Joy* is the sum and substance of emotional health, trusting God in all things.

- *Compassion* keeps you deeply concerned about others. No selfish ambition or vain conceit.

- *Confidence* allows you to emphatically trust God and believe he has great plans for your life, regardless of what is happening now.

- *Contentment* allows you to be thankful for much or little, spending no time and energy comparing your lot in life to others.

"The seeds of depression, anger and resentment cannot take root in a grateful heart."
—Andy Andrews, *7 Decisions of Personal Success*

Stamp Collecting Exercise

A story I heard from David Sandler asks us to imagine each negative emotion as a coupon book, like the old S&H Green Stamps people received at their local grocery stores—similar to today's computer-generated bonus points on shopping receipts. Each coupon book contains numerous stamps or points with certain values to accumulate and redeem for various items or discounts.

Using the Stamp Collecting exercise, place each negative stamp—like anger, guilt, bitterness, or shame—in its respective coupon book. Each book requires a long time to complete before it can be redeemed. So instead of dealing with negative emotions when they occur, you suppress them by placing individual stamps in the book until one day you can hopefully "redeem" your pent-up emotion on an unsuspecting person—who probably was not the one you were bitter with in the first place.

Remember the principle that when you get emotionally involved in the situation, you get killed? With negative stamp collecting, the redemption kills two people.

Fear Immobilizes Productive Action

Since the emotion of fear grips us on a regular basis, God gave us 366 separate scriptures in the Bible—one for each day of the year plus an extra for leap year—to fear not, fret not, worry not, and to be anxious for nothing! He did this because he knew we would need daily reminders in order to live a fearless, courageous, and balanced life.

In reality, most fears never come to pass. One of my favorite quotes comes from Mark Twain: "I have experienced many terrible things in life, some of which actually happened." We can also use FEAR as an acronym—False Evidence Appearing Real.

Instead of fear, it is faith which leads to emotional health. We already understand that the way we think is a powerful weapon. Your most powerful weapon to defeat fear and worry is that faith.

During the COVID-19 pandemic, Rick Warren offered a list of Ten Commandments for emotional health:

- Show grace to myself and others.
- Start and end each day, refueling my soul.
- Set and stick with a simple routine.
- Stop watching so much news.
- Schedule a daily connection with people you love.

- Share your feelings instead of stuffing or stamp collecting them.
- Seek advice before making major decisions.
- Space renewal breaks throughout your day.
- Serve someone suffering more than you.
- Control the controllable and trust God for the rest.

Biblical truths defeat unreal fear and lies. Romans 8:28 says: "And we know that God causes everything to work together for the good of those who love God and are called according to his purpose for them."

Remember, everything we ever want in life is on the other side of fear. Whatever you fear the most, when you address that fear, it becomes your greatest asset.

Winners behave themselves out of fear and into a good attitude.

Building Emotional Strength

It is important to build your emotional strength so that you can overcome the negative feelings or joy-stealers that deplete your energy and minimize your potential for happiness.

Emotional strength entails three emotional muscles:

1. Emotional resiliency
2. Emotional control
3. Emotional toughness

Emotional strength fuels your capacity to experience the fullness of life without the disruption of prolonged bouts of negativity.

Gray attitudes become the exception, not the expectation. With emotional strength, "down" moments are viewed in the light of truth and acknowledged for what they really are. Emotional strength is not about denying your problems. It is about acknowledging a fear, a greater power, a far greater power, affirming God rather than affirming your woes.

The foundation of emotional strength is mental wellbeing. When you focus your thoughts on what is noble and right, as in the *4:8 Principle* by Tommy Newberry, you develop your mental muscle. Without this mental muscle, you will inevitably experience cracks in your "foundation" that will frustrate your efforts at living a joy-filled life.

You can control your thoughts; therefore, you can significantly improve your emotional strength, including, of course, your potential for joy. Our feelings seldom provide reliable advice for decision making. Much of the world would have you believe otherwise. Popular culture encourages us to follow our feelings, even though emotions can swiftly cloud our ability to make wise decisions, or choices that we will be proud of when all is said and done. The Bible tells us that the heart or feelings are not to be trusted. "Guard your heart above all else, for it determines the course of your life."[22]

Jeremiah 17:9-10 says: "The human heart is the most deceitful of all things, and desperately wicked. Who really knows how bad it is? But I, the Lord, search all hearts and examine secret motives. I give all people their due rewards, according to what their actions deserve."

You won't find this biblical truth in any Hallmark movie that tells everyone to "just follow your heart."

---

[22] Proverbs 4:23.

The Laws of Emotional Strength

In order to get control of your emotional life, you must understand three principles that explain the mental dynamics of emotional health:

1. The Law of Attention

Whatever you dwell upon becomes top of mind awareness for you. For example, the more you emphasize your good health with both silent thoughts and public speech, the healthier you feel. The more you stay mindful of positive qualities in your spouse, the closer and stronger your relationship will become. The more attention you give your kids, the more influence you will have in their lives. The more you mull over God's promises, the greater your spiritual convictions become.

Alternatively, the more you mentally replay a particular injustice, the more frustrated you will become. Your emotional life can advance only after your negative thoughts retreat. You will always feel what you dwell on.

If your emotional life today is not where you ultimately want it to be, then your top priority should be shifting your attention to your blessings, to your strengths, and to the aspects of your life that are working. Resist the urge to accelerate negative emotional spirals by chronically reporting your own negative headlines. Stop talking so much about your mistakes, setbacks, and disappointments.

Refuse to fuel negative emotions by constantly talking about what is wrong with your marriage, your oldest kid, your sore back, your strange neighbors, or the world in general.

Instead, broadcast your blessings to anyone who will listen, verbalize your vision for the future to trusted friends and allies, turn the spotlight of your concentration to your future hopes and dreams, to the grand and mysterious future that God has in store for you.

"For I know the plans I have for you," says the Lord. "They are plans for good and not for disaster, to give you a future and a hope."[23]

The flipside of this law of attention is that whatever you stop thinking about or turn your attention away from tends to atrophy and drop out of your life. Starve worry, fear, and doubt by no longer nourishing them with your attention. Remember, what you focus on, you are going to experience. If you have an urge to go negative, know that it will not produce anything positive.

2. The Law of Exchange

This simply means that you can do away with a negative thought only when you replace it with a positive thought. If you like, you can also purge positive thoughts by substituting them with negative thoughts. I don't know why anyone would want to do that, but that option, as you've probably observed, is widely practiced. Your conscious mind can hold only one thought at a time, and that one thought is either in alignment with your potential for joy or it is not. This is good news because it means you can swap an average thought with a brilliant one, or a fearful thought with a courageous one whenever you choose.

However, you cannot eliminate a thought by fighting it or trying to block it out. Resisting an unwanted thought only entangles the issue, and drives that thought deeper into your mind, making it even more of a distraction. Release the need to hang on to thoughts that haven't worked well in your life.

---

[23] Jeremiah 29:11.

If you want to gain emotional control, you first have to gain mental control.

3. The Law of Reversibility

This simply refers to your God-installed capability to evoke feelings as a result of deliberate behavior. One of the most effective and least utilized methods for upgrading your emotional life is acting your way into the feelings you most desire. If you're not experiencing as much joy, passion, or satisfaction as you would like, you can, over time, act your way into those higher emotions by behaving and thinking in ways consistent with your emotional goal. Most people resist this option because they have been conditioned to believe that positive emotions should happen naturally. Some people reason that if you have to work at it, it's not genuine; it is not authentic. If it is authentic, it should be automatic, right?

I can understand these reactions, but one thing is certain. If you were to rule out the option of acting into your feelings, you will forever be doomed to enjoy only those positive emotions that arise spontaneously. However, once you've decided that following scripture and fulfilling your potential dictates a particular choice, then acting your way into feelings is simply the discipline that will align your behavior with your values. God has built this power for personal change into all of us, even though it may not feel comfortable right away.

To those who feel as if they're lying when they act better than they feel, let me say that there is a far greater likelihood that negative emotions, not positive ones, are rooted in untruth.

To illustrate the Law of Reversibility, think of a time when you initially didn't feel like doing something. Most people can relate to occasionally waking up and feeling pretty lousy.

However, within a few minutes of being up and about, they feel absolutely fine even without caffeine. This is the Law of Reversibility in action.

As another example, almost everyone has experienced the intention to exercise without an accompanying feeling of enthusiasm. I know I have! I've learned to push through this wall by getting myself moving. Just changing into my workout clothes keeps the momentum going. Then warming up moves me a little closer to the feeling I'm after. Once I'm on the treadmill or elliptical, I almost feel like exercising. And within 10-15 minutes I am embarrassed that I came so close to blowing off my workout. I forced myself to act in a manner consistent with my values, not in a manner consistent with my feelings at that particular moment.

Winners behave themselves into a good attitude.

Vulnerability Is Not a Weakness[24]

As we continue to explore the Emotional area, on your journey to becoming the healthy, authentic person you were created to be, understand that being vulnerable is not a weakness. This stands contrary to worldview messages we are exposed to from all corners of society, but James 4:6 says: "God opposes the proud but gives grace to the humble." Your vulnerability is not a weakness... in fact, your vulnerability is a strength! God uses our vulnerabilities to spiritually empower us, to emotionally heal us, to make us relationally attractive, and formed for leadership.

Being open and honest with others about our weaknesses is spiritually empowering because it opens the door to God's

[24] https://pastorrick.com/four-strengths-in-vulnerability/

grace. Grace is the power you need to change and break through your bad habits and weaknesses.

Vulnerability is also emotionally healing. James 5:16 says: "Confess your sins to each other and pray for each other so that you may be healed. The earnest prayer of a righteous person has great power and produces wonderful results." To simply be forgiven, you don't need to confess your sin to anyone other than God. But to be truly healed, you've got to share your weaknesses with somebody else. Revealing your feelings is the beginning of healing.

Vulnerability is relationally attractive. The Bible says, "Indeed, we all make many mistakes."[25] When someone reveals that they make mistakes too, they become more relatable. By admitting weaknesses, you can actually draw people in.

Being vulnerable is also a requirement for leadership. "Humble yourselves before the Lord and he will lift you up in honor."[26] God honors your humility and vulnerability and uses them to form you into a leader.

The Bible can really be countercultural. The world tells you to keep your guard up and not appear weak, but God says to boast in your weaknesses because they reveal his power and make you more dependent upon him.[27]

Will you let your guard down so that your weaknesses can point others to Jesus Christ?

Admit–Commit–Submit

As always, the challenge is yours to respond.

---

[25] James 3:2.
[26] James 4:10.
[27] II Corinthians 12:9.

- What worldview thinking regarding your emotional health are you ready to *admit* to that is negatively impacting your Balance Wheel?

- What biblical values are you ready to *commit* to pursuing to replace negative, hurtful emotions you have allowed to control your emotional health?

- Who are you prepared to *submit* to for regular accountability regarding your new commitments to replace hurtful emotions with more positive and helpful emotions?

Challenge

Name your Top 3 Emotions to *decrease* in the next year:

-

-

-

Name your Top 3 Emotions to *increase* in the next year:

-

-

-

When I personally took this challenge on February 10, 2016, I decided to decrease the emotions of fatigue, overload, and exhaustion, while also deciding to increase the emotions of drive, awe, and energy. I am extremely happy to report that five years later, on October 30, 2021, at age 71, the improvement in each of these emotional goals continues to resonate throughout all areas of my Balance Wheel. So there is no excuse that anyone is too old to change!

Closing Scripture

"I saw the Lord and he answered me. He delivered me from all my fears." (Psalm 34:4)

"Fearing people is a dangerous trap, but trusting the Lord means safety." (Proverbs 29:25)

"Don't be afraid, for I am with you. Don't be discouraged, for I am your God. I will strengthen you and help you. I will hold you up with my victorious right hand." (Isaiah 41:10)

"I am leaving you with a gift—peace of mind and heart. And the peace I give is a gift the world cannot give. So do not be troubled or afraid." (John 14:27)

"I will greet this day with a forgiving spirit.
Today, I will choose to be happy!"
—Andy Andrews, 7 Decisions of Personal Success

---

7 | SOCIAL/PERSONAL

Choosing and developing strong relationships

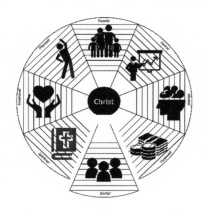

As we continue to dissect the Balance Wheel areas, I have decided to pair Social with Personal. They are inter-connected and contain many of the differentiators that distinguish those few highly successful, balanced, and emotionally strong individuals from others who live mediocre, unbalanced, and emotionally drained lives.

The social area entails pressure from the battle taking place in our minds regarding superior intellect versus social skills. Social pressures can negatively impact relationships.

Second, we will dive into the area of scripts that negatively impact personal growth, our relationships, and our ability to live effectively, like the top 10% of highly successful people.

Third, we will introduce core competencies and crucial elements of success for social skills development that are available to everyone who is fed up, living in the past, playing the victim role, and making excuses for a lack of success, fulfillment, and overall life balance.

Prior to this deeper dive, be reminded that two forces will have the greatest positive or negative impact on personal and professional success:

1. What you allow to go into your mind, whether it be what you read, view, or listen to

2. The people you decide to associate with

In life, how well we navigate is also dependent in large part on the quality and character of our friends. Those we choose—our trusted inner circle—can make or break us, and we can in turn make or break them.

You must make the shift to investing time with the right people, individuals who lift you up and produce a godly return in your life. How exactly do you determine which people are the right ones to invite into your inner circle? Well, it all depends on your particular vision, but if your aim is a joy-filled life, here are seven thought triggers to get you started.

Invest More Time with People Who Look Like This:

1. Their character and integrity are equal to or greater than your own.

2. They share your faith, or even better, they are further along in their relationship with God.

3. Their lives demonstrate that joy-filled fruit of their faith.

4. You'd like your children to grow up and be similar to them.

5. They hold you accountable and ask you the tough questions that are avoided by the majority.

6. They draw the best out of you and remind you that God is doing exciting things through you.

7. They are sincerely committed to being positively sharpened by their exposure to you.

Have too many friends? That sounds a bit odd. Can you ever have too many friends? After all, isn't life all about relationships? The answer is both yes and no.

The key is to have an inner circle of close friends with whom you have developed trust over time. These are your go-to people, the ones you can count on to be honest with you, no matter what. Even Jesus, within his group of 12 disciples, had an inner circle of just three—Peter, James, and John—with whom he had a deeper level of trust and closeness.

When you let too many into that inner circle, it can devalue the most important friendships. Wise friends help us navigate life successfully. Being a wise friend brings life to others as well. "A person of many companions may come to ruin, but there is a friend who sticks closer than a brother."[28]

Explaining the Social Area

Wisdom Walks: 40 Life Principles for a Significant and Meaningful Journey is one of my annual reads along my pursuit of wisdom. It begins with the principle that: "Your words are powerful and permanent." (This will make even more sense later in this chapter when we discuss Life Scripts.)

Chances are, sometimes you've said something you wish you could take back. I know I sure have. When our words hurt

---

[28] Proverbs 18:24, *ESV.*

someone we care deeply about, we wish we could reel them back in, like they were attached to a fishing line. Maybe that quiet voice in the mind was busy warning us, "Don't say it," or "You're going to regret this." Still, we find ourselves unable to hold our tongues.

The old adage "Sticks and stones may break my bones, but words will never hurt me" simply isn't true. Often times those hurtful, discouraging words are remembered decades later.

Today's technology has created a platform to instantly broadcast our every thought or feeling. Texting, email, websites and social media platforms like Facebook and Twitter have totally transformed the ways we communicate. Twitter has become so popular that if you're not "tweeting," eyes roll to tell you you're missing out. You can tweet that you're bored and eating ice cream as long as you use 140 characters or less.

But when you start to read some of the stuff that's being tweeted and how it instantly makes its way around the world into headlines and onto talk shows, it's easy to realize how careful you have to be with your words. These tweets can't be taken back, and they're instantly forwarded from one end of the Earth to the other.

All these communications create a powerful permanent record. People have lost jobs over things they've said through email. Others have ended relationships with a text message. Athletes openly disagree with decisions of their coaches and team owners. And now colleges and employers review applicants' online identities when considering them for admissions or employment. Untold damage is being done by improperly expressing our words for the whole world to see.[29]

The worldview says "more is better." We now have a generation of all ages who incorrectly assess their social skills on the basis of Followers, Contacts, and Likes, while unable to sign their name or hold a meaningful and effective conversation with another human being.

Compare that approach to factors attributed as foundational to social and financial success by the highly successful and balanced multi-millionaires included in the *Millionaire Mind* by Dr. Thomas J. Stanley.

Overwhelmingly, they credit these top factors for their life balance and success:

1. Integrity—being honest with all people

2. Discipline—applying self-control

3. Social skills—getting along with people

4. Home life—having a supportive spouse

5. Hard work—more than most people accomplish

Notice that all five factors are either EQ (Emotional Intelligence) or AQ (Adversity Quotient) rather than IQ (superior intellect) characteristics.

Your Personal Life Scripts

In this next section, you will identify life scripts that either help or hinder your personal growth, and discover how they have a positive or negative impact on building strong

---

[29]   https://www.forbes.com/sites/alicegwalton/2017/06/30/a-run-down-of-social-medias-effects-on-our-mental-health/?sh=6024ce542e5a

relationships. Then we will review the core competencies for social relationship skills development.

Throughout our *Life of Balance* journey together, I have attempted to help you discover whether you are satisfied or dissatisfied with your Life Wheel, and if not, to provide you a new way of thinking and behaving in order to finish your life race in a meaningful way, similar to how the 10% of highly successful people have lived.

Consider how much time you have left on this earth. I will now explain the primary difference between the 10% and the 90%. The difference is that the 10% never look backward— except to learn lessons from past failures. Rather, they look and press forward, dropping their self-limiting head trash.

Philippians 3:13-14 says: "Brothers and sisters, I focus on one thing: Forgetting the past and looking forward to what lies ahead."

The 90%, however, spend all their time looking backward from their present to birth, rehashing the guilt, disappointments, complaints, excuses, comparisons, anger, and all other negative thoughts and results that they have *absolutely no control over to change...* the 10% focuses only on what they can control—their own thoughts and actions.

The answer and choice is yours alone to make... to drop the head trash and unproductive life scripts that have been holding you back from living a life of balance and success.

For those who decide to drop the head trash, please know that your current and past sphere of influencers—those who are responsible for placing much of those negative and unproductive scripts in your mind—will undoubtedly come after you with a vengeance. But just like you would never think of bringing your household stinking garbage and trash back into your clean house, it is entirely up to you to say no to those who want you to hold on to negative, unproductive, and stinking thinking of your past imbalanced life.

To help you further identify those hurtful, unhelpful scripts, revisit the Mental and Emotional Balance Wheel life areas (chapters 4 and 6) and consider how that scripting impacts your transactions and relationships with others.

Core Competencies for Social Relationships & Skills Development

Transactional analysis (TA)

Simply stated, transactional analysis (TA) provides an understanding and model for conducting moment by moment transactions between humans, by determining which ego state we are communicating from.

Each ego state represents recordings or messages which contain *every thought and feeling* we have been exposed to since birth. All of these messages have formed the basis of our life scripts, and subsequently impact our transactions with everyone we come into contact with. These recordings are broken down into the following files:

1. **Parent ego state**—made up of two conflicting recordings

    a. *Critical Parent.* Expressed with harsh messages of the do's and don'ts of life

    b. *Nurturing Parent.* Emotionally soothing, supportive messages on the do's and don'ts

2. **Adult ego state**—Calm, logical, fact-driven, and objective messages

3. **Child ego state**—These are the feelings about the parental messages, and come from three different childlike emotions:

   a. *The Natural Child.* The life of the party, their motto is to just have fun.

   b. *The Adaptive Child.* They do whatever they're told to do because they don't want to disappoint anyone.

   c. *The Rebellious Child.* They do the opposite of what they're told to do, because life is not fair.

What these ego states represent are the answers to our conversation in Chapter 6 on the Emotional area. Remember the Sandler principle, "When you get emotionally involved in the situation, you get killed"? Getting killed in this sense is when you speak and act like a critical, harsh parent who is always pointing the finger at weaknesses and failures versus the nurturing parent who makes certain to protect the intrinsic value as a human being while addressing failures and areas to improve.

"Getting killed" is also what happens when we use our child ego state messages to whine, manipulate, and rebel against any attempt to deal with role failures and limitations. A simple, but not necessarily easy, way to keep us from reverting to using critical parent and child responses is to remember to use our nurturing parent ego state 70% of the time in communications, and an adult ego state 30% of the time, especially when attempting to deal with conflict or failure to achieve desired results. We call this having an Adult/Adult Transaction, regardless of the ages or experience of those involved in the communication transaction.[30]

Separating Your Internal Values from Your External Actions

Highly successful, balanced people know the difference between their intrinsic value as a human being and their extrinsic actions and results.

As a life and business coach for nearly forty years, I consider inside/outside change—separating how your internal value impacts your external actions—as opposed to your social influences, as the most critical element, a lynchpin to real life change and all practical growth and development.

Pay particular and serious attention as we discuss the differences between how people compare themselves to others. After working with people from every business discipline and walk of life, it has been and continues to be my greatest privilege to watch them grow and outperform their competitors, once they understand and accept their value as *human beings* versus *human doings*.

Many people relate their self-worth—self-identity, self-esteem, or self-image—to their outward performance. If they have performed particularly well doing a certain action or achieving a certain outcome, they feel good about themselves, as though they have more worth. If they didn't do well, they don't feel good about themselves and in turn feel like they are worth less—not just as a human doing, but as a human being. For these people, their self-worth is shaped by their successes and failures in their various roles.

---

[30] You can find much more practical help and information on TA in: *You Can't Teach a Kid to Ride a Bike at a Seminar,* by David H. Sandler, and *Sandler Success Principles* by David Mattson and Bruce Seidman.

Over time, they develop a self-worth image ranging from very low to very high. Why did they make that connection?

Abilities

When you were born, you had no conscious abilities. You were just you. As you grew, your parents and others began to assign to you various identities—like daughter or son, brother or sister, student, friend, playmate. You continued to increase other areas of focus throughout your life as you formed new relationships like marriage, and tried new activities at work and in your leisure time.

Every identity has rules or expectations that define what constitutes good performance. Good children obey their parents. Good students get high grades. Good salespeople close big sales.

Most of the time you'll find that the praise and rewards you receive are connected to your results achieved. The same is true of the criticism and penalties. When you cleaned your room, your mom rewarded you with a hug and perhaps a cookie. You earned her acceptance not simply for being you, but instead by completing the task of cleaning your room.

When you received good grades, your parents praised you and colleges offered you a scholarship. Your teacher probably didn't report to your parents that in addition to having an aptitude for math, you had a healthy sense of your own worth. When you hit a winning home run in a softball game, your friends and teammates commented on it for days afterward. They probably never complimented you for just being yourself.

This type of feedback from parents, teachers, bosses, and so on, is how you came to believe that your intrinsic value depended on how well you performed in your activities. If you confuse your role performance with your value as a human being, your self-image will inevitably suffer. After all, you won't excel at everything you try to do. No one does.

High achievers are people who consistently rate their intrinsic value very high. That is, they have high self-esteem and feel good about themselves regardless of their actions and results. They don't need success to validate their self-worth and they don't allow failure to devalue it. Their self-esteem comes from within. High achievers are willing to take risks and try something new or do things differently. They recognize the outcome of such activities as just that... an outcome, and nothing more. Sometimes the outcome will be favorable; sometimes it won't. In both cases, they accept responsibility, and neither case will affect how they view their value as a human being.

At the other end of the scale are the *low achievers*. They consistently rate their intrinsic value very low. Low achievers have low self-esteem. They tend to have little confidence in their abilities and judgment. They don't expect to win and most often they don't. Low achievers are unlikely to try something new or do things differently. After all, if they try something new and don't obtain favorable results, it only reinforces the poor image they already held of themselves. And when low achievers do experience failure, they look for excuses on which to blame the poor result. If they failed to close the sale, for instance, they might blame the economy. Not accepting responsibility defeats positive outcomes as well. If a low achiever closes a big or particularly difficult sale, he or she will attribute it to luck. Low achievers tend to feel victimized by both good and bad luck. They often resent others for whom success appears to come more easily.

Then there are those who view themselves as *mediocre*, where the vast number of human beings see themselves.

Their intrinsic value is heavily dependent on their life results. They don't stretch outside their comfort zone to strive for greater levels of success. They settle for "safe" and "status quo" in order to feel good about themselves.

Regardless of how you view yourself, you will discover that your level of success in life is directly connected to the intrinsic value you feel.

Your mental image of yourself acts like a performance gauge, regulating your actions. Just like a thermostat controls room temperature, your mental image sets upper and lower limits on the quality of your performance within each area of your life, as well as your life as a whole.

You can walk over to the wall and change the thermostat any time you want—if you are willing to do it. But because your self-image is wired to your short-term emotional appetite, you will hardly ever feel like acting in a manner inconsistent with this self-image set-point.

However, there is a solution! You can override past negative programing by deliberately choosing new behaviors that align with your God-given potential, whether or not you feel like it.

Your self-image, or inner mirror, determines how you use your time, talents, knowledge, skills, and experiences. Did you catch that last sentence? It explains one of the great mysteries of life. Why do many gifted and often well-educated individuals fail to live up to their potential? In more cases than we might like to acknowledge, it is because they see themselves as low achievers instead of high achievers. We all know lots of folks who have great talent but do little with it. In the same vein, we know plenty of people who have few advantages but who make the most of them.

Recognize the true source

Legitimate, lasting self-worth can come only from God's love, from knowing and experiencing who you are as a new creation in Christ. See yourself as a child of God. You are God's special enterprise! Work to recognize that fact emotionally, not just intellectually. If you keep thinking of yourself the way you used to be, that is exactly what you will continue to be.

Too many people base their self-worth on what others think about them. But if you depend on others for your self-worth, is it even accurate to call it self-worth? Beware of making a god of other people's opinions. Needing approval from others is an immobilizing trap. It is essentially saying that someone else's opinion of you is more important than God's.

It may be helpful in certain situations to remind yourself quietly, *"What you think of me is none of my business."*

When you stay focused on God's promises, you realize that you have already been approved. Authentic self-worth is intrinsic. It comes from within, not from acquisitions, accolades, or approval from others. Despite any shortcomings, weaknesses, or blunders, God loves you.

Agree with your creator. He knows everything about you, and still loves you. Your love for yourself should mirror that love. This is critical because you will only receive what, deep down, you believe you are worthy of having.

Any permanent progress in life starts on the inside and spreads to the outside. Attempted improvements that begin externally are doomed for failure in the long run. Why? All lasting growth begins with changes to the mental images you hold inside your head. They ultimately spread to the outside and create permanent changes in your circumstances. This is part of God's perfect design.

Much discouragement and underachievement result from dwelling on the failings of our human nature. A mediocre self-concept does not come from God but from the stains of the world. It comes from seeing ourselves differently from how God sees us. It results from continuing to identify with and claim the things that haven't worked. It comes from not acknowledging or forgetting the value placed on us by the creator of the universe.

When you remind yourself of your true identity, you will also find it much easier to live a life of excellence and filter out the junk that steals your joy. When you see yourself as a child of God, you do not accept artificial restrictions on the quantity of joy or the level of impact you can have in this world. That's critical because how you perceive yourself sets the ceiling for what God can do with you.

When you see yourself as down and defeated, that is what you will surely be. This woeful approach does you no good personally and only serves to minimize your contribution in the world. *Again, the choice is yours...* either to accept what the world says about your value or what God says about your value.

Core Competencies of Those Who Accept God's Value

These people regularly exhibit the following attitudes and behaviors of accountability and vulnerability, which lead to successful and balanced lives.

Positive Attitudes:

1. About self
2. About learning

3. About growing
4. About the value they bring to others

Takes Responsibility:

1. Doesn't externalize or blame others or their past
2. Knows it's up to them
3. Knows the only things that can be controlled are their own activity and behavior
4. Knows it's OK to fail

Doesn't Need Approval of Others:

1. Has strong self-confidence
2. High self-image
3. Is not affected by what others think
4. Realizes there is a lot to learn and it's OK not to be perfect

Supportive Beliefs:

1. OK to hear "No"
2. OK not to get approval
3. Has self-image of 10 (on a scale of 1-10)

Controls Emotions:

1. Doesn't take things personally
2. Knows what to say or do at the appropriate time

Recovers from Rejection:

1. It doesn't affect their self-image
2. Understands they aren't being rejected personally
3. Willing to put themselves in high-risk situations
4. Puts last engagement quickly behind them

Effective Listening/Questioning:

1. Helps others do the talking

2. Knows what questions to ask
3. Ask lots of how and why questions
4. Doesn't get emotionally involved

Although there are additional core competencies and pinpointed behaviors regarding knowledge and skills, development, and proficiency, the high achievers are too busy pursuing their *Good to Great to Significance* journey to be held back or derailed by the majority who tell them they are not worthy enough to have what it takes to be successful.

Admit—Commit—Submit

- What worldview thinking are you ready to *admit* to that is negatively impacting your acceptance of your God-given identity as a human being?

- What biblical view are you ready to *commit* to pursuing to replace negative and ineffective ways of thinking regarding your value as a human being?

- Who are you prepared to *submit* to for regular accountability regarding your new commitments on thinking differently and pursuit of highly successful core competencies and behaviors?

Closing Scripture

"Don't copy the behavior and customs of this world, but let God transform you into a new person by changing the way you think. Then you will learn to know God's will for you, which is good, pleasing and perfect." (Romans 12:2)

"Love prospers when a fault is forgiven, but dwelling on it separates close friends." (Proverbs 17:9)

"A man of many companions may come to ruin, but there is a friend who sticks closer than a brother." (Proverbs 18:24, ESV)

"Then Jesus told them, 'A prophet is honored everywhere except in his own hometown and among his relatives and his own family'." (Mark 6:4)

Thought to Remember

If the world rejected its Creator and Savior, we don't have a chance that we won't be rejected as well throughout life. But just like Jesus overcame this world and death, he gives all who call on his strength the help to achieve everything we were created to accomplish.

8 | FINANCIAL

No amount of money can buy a balanced life

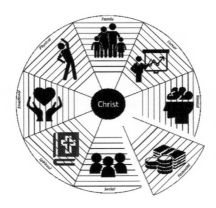

The intent of this book is to challenge your thinking and behavior in every area of the Life Wheel. In this chapter we will open your awareness to the consequences of violating simple economic principles. You will answer life's tough money questions, and learn practical steps to plan for your financial freedom.

So whether you have an annual income of less than a thousand dollars or hundreds of thousands of dollars, our conversation still revolves around the tremendous emotional, mental, social, family, and physical stresses experienced by the human race due to a lack of understanding and application of proven biblical principles.

I promise, regardless of whether you are a child or senior citizen, that we will address your challenges and provide hope for an economically balanced and financially fulfilling future.

Dave Ramsey's Financial Peace University is a proven resource for practical improvement regarding a biblical plan for financial freedom. Zero investment or tax advice is provided, just simple steps to enable everyone to bring more balance to their economic area of their Balance Wheel.[31]

As you continue to read, you will discover from my personal story, that regardless of your background or current economic messes, incredible improvement can be achieved, both in the short and long term, provided you take 100% responsibility for your economic condition.

Much of what you learned about life scripts will come into play as we discuss the achievement of economic balance, especially those in the U.S. who are bombarded with income equality and entitlement messages without corresponding messages pertaining to personal responsibility and individual initiative. Remember, until you change the way you think, it is impossible to change your performance and results.

Relationship Between Courage and Wealth

Dr. Thomas Stanley outlines what it takes to break the cycle of economic achievement in your own generation. No amount of money can buy a balanced life. His research proves this beyond a shadow of a doubt as he identifies the differences between two categories of Economic Affluence.

The first he calls the Income Statement Affluent (the "Spenders"). They have an annual household income of between $300k-$750k+.

A high percentage of the "Spenders" have the following to show for their annual high incomes:

---

[31] Visit http://DaveRamsey.com/FPU to get started.

- Low to zero net worth
- Credit dependency
- Controlled by others
- Jumbo mortgages resulting in heavy debt
- Low to zero savings

Ecclesiastes 5:10 says: "Those who love money will never have enough. How meaningless to think that wealth brings true happiness." And I Timothy 6:10 says: "For the love of money is the root of all kinds of evil. And some people, craving money, have wandered from the true faith and pierced themselves with many sorrows."

Next are the Balance Sheet Affluent (the "Savers"):

- Very high net worth
- Very low to zero debt
- Substantial savings

In the above cases, both the "Spenders" and the "Savers" create high levels of annual income, ranking in the top few percent of the entire world's population of over seven billion people. So having enough money is not the problem! The extreme difference is in their thinking and daily habits.

The "Spenders" exhibit extreme cases of unbalanced life wheels, while the vast majority of the "Savers" experience life wheels that are highly balanced.

Using Dr. Stanley's *Millionaire Mind* research, anyone can see the "Spenders" mostly focus on themselves, with life activities built around consumption of the next promise of happiness. In contrast, the majority of "Savers" experience high levels of balance and happiness because the bulk of their thinking and daily activities are focused on serving and giving to others.

The following list ranks their respective activities. Examine it to discover the vast differences which produce polar opposite Balance Wheels. These lifestyle activities clearly illustrate the differences between "Me"-focused Spenders and "Others"-focused Savers.

"Spenders"

- Purchase or plan to purchase expensive automobiles, technologies and other must-have toys

- Dine at expensive restaurants

- Shop at high-end clothing stores like Saks Fifth Avenue, Brooks Brothers, Nordstrom's, and Neiman Marcus

- Ski in the Rockies or Alps

- Sail on a yacht

- Gamble at casinos

- Take an ocean cruise around the world

- Attend a grand slam tennis tournament

All these activities lead to a group of people who are overspent, overfed, overdressed, over liquored, over traveled, over entertained, overindulgent in general, and who have very imbalanced life wheels.

Proverbs 13:7 says: "Some who are poor pretend to be rich; others who are rich pretend to be poor." Proverbs 11:28 reinforces, "Trust in your money and down you go! But the godly flourish like leaves in spring!"

"Savers"

- Socialize with children and grandchildren

- Entertain close friends

- Plan investments

- Study investment opportunities

- Take photographs

- Watch children and grandchildren play their sports

- Consult with an investment adviser

- Attend religious services

- Jog/run

- Pray and read the Bible

Overall, these regular activities lead to greater happiness, fulfillment, and more balanced life wheels.

While I recognize that most will never achieve millionaire or multi-millionaire status, the fact is that regardless of income levels, it is possible to emulate the behaviors of the "Savers" to experience a balanced life of affluence.

A 2019 *Forbes* article states that 9 out of 10 people are one fiscal surprise away from financial trouble, one paycheck away from financial ruin. Between 70-90% of people say they are not happy with their lives, including those who are wealthy. Why is this the case? What does God's word say about why this happens? And most importantly what can you do about it?

Your Current Economic Reality

First, let's take an honest and comprehensive look at your current fiscal reality.

This initial step is to determine how serious you are about taking control of your money for good, by determining what is most important. You do this by recognizing that your biggest wealth-building tool is your income, and the best way to harness the power of that income is through a monthly budget. Investing and saving for college are important items, but it's the monthly budget from which everything else becomes possible.

Want to invest money in a mutual fund? Make room for that allocation in the monthly budget. Want to get out of debt? List your debts in your spending plan.

You get the idea. The sad thing is that lots of people rank making and following a budget only slightly more enticing than acquiring the Black Plague. Budgeting, to them, means no fun, bread-and-water for every meal, and custom-fitted straightjackets. What they don't realize is that a spending plan is the fastest way to take control of your finances and get out of debt.

Many people don't make a budget because they are afraid of what they will find out if they have overspent to the point of facing a mountain of debt, with little or no savings. They might be shamed into stopping right there. Don't fall into that trap!

If you find yourself battling such resistance and fears about the practice of creating and adhering to a daily, weekly, or monthly budget, I encourage you to consider Dave Ramsey's Financial Peace University. Through video courses, class discussions, and small-group activities, Financial Peace University offers practical steps to get from where you are to where you have dreamed. This plan will show you how to eliminate debt, manage your money, and spend and save wisely.

You can make a budget any way that works for you. It might be just a yellow pad and pen, which is the method I started with over 50 years ago, or maybe it's a spreadsheet. You might choose Dave Ramsey's budget forms or the helpful Gazelle Budget tool. You pick your favorite.

You must make a new budget for each month. Every time that calendar flips, there are new birthdays, holidays, insurance bills, tax refunds, gas bills, life events, and so on. There is no such thing as a perfect budget that works the same for every month. If you want to win with money, you've got to do the details. Every month you must revisit your budget to gain control of your money so you can build wealth.

As you begin to reduce debt and accumulate wealth, consider these seven "baby steps":

1. Develop a $1,000 emergency fund

2. Pay off all debts, smallest to largest

3. Create a fully funded emergency fund to cover 3-6 months of expenses

4. Invest 15% of pretax income in retirement savings

5. Invest for kids' college tuition

6. Pay off the house

7. Build wealth and give a bunch away

You make it all work. When it comes down to sticking to the budget, it is ultimately up to you. It means getting up each day, going to work, coming home, and not spending money that you haven't budgeted. There is no magic formula to making this work. Each day you make your choices. The budget works when you do.

If you make a spending plan that includes paying off debt, saving for emergencies, investing (when the time is right), and paying off the house, and then you stick to it month after month, your situation will get better in every sense of the word. It's like following a map to buried treasure. You will discover the most direct route to riches... and learn the places to avoid.

The budget is your treasure map. The treasure is waiting. So go get it!

My Personal Budget Story

For those of you who are skeptical or fearful that something so simple (remember, I did not say *easy*) could be so effective, regardless of current economic conditions or age, I offer my unvarnished, no exaggerated four-generation budget story. It involves my personal journey with my wife, Tibby, our children now ages 42, 48 and 50, and our seven grandchildren, ages 18 to 27, and my mother, a single mom who raised seven kids and passed six years ago, less than three months shy of 90 years old.

A little personal background may provide perspective and validity to my assertions that anyone can achieve a balanced life, provided they are willing to take 100% responsibility and remain accountable and vulnerable to others.

I started working in the neighborhood by age five, shoveling snow, mowing lawns, and mucking horse stalls. At age eight I was awarded a trip to the 1958 New York World's Fair after selling 100 Sunday subscriptions to the *Harrisburg/York Patriot News,* to bring my total to 128 customers, spanning five miles from one end of my hometown to the other.

In those days, you delivered papers on Sunday and collected payment during the week. Sunday deliveries began at 5:30 A.M. and finished by 11:30 A.M. Collections took at least 10 hours each week for a total of 16-20 hours, for the grand average of around $8 per week, or about $0.40-0.50 per hour.

By ninth and tenth grades, I was washing dishes at the diner on Friday and Saturday nights from 11:00 P.M. to 7:00 A.M. for $1 an hour. During my senior year in high school, I worked as a short order cook 40-50 hours a week at $1.50 per hour.

I share these details not to bemoan the hard work, inconveniences, or low income. I was already wealthy compared to my other six siblings until they were able to find jobs. But I remember the life lessons taught by the four local business owners and executives who took me under their wings. Those lessons prepared me for every aspect of selling and management leadership. They ultimately led me to a 50-year business career encompassing 20 years in sales and management with two of the nation's largest trucking companies, which prepared me for the last 31 years of building a Sandler Training franchise from zero during the 1990 recession.

Married at age 19, my wife Tibby and I began budgeting immediately. We were disciplined to only buy something if we had the money to pay for it. Our budget dealt with priorities—obligations like rent, furniture, and car payments—and necessities like food and gas. I personally did the grocery shopping for our first six years, which included the births of our son Bob and daughter Kelly. As soon as they were able to sit in the shopping cart, they came with me. Without exception, I shopped our grocery list of meats, milk, bread, eggs, and butter, and when my subtotal reached the budget number, I stopped shopping and went to the checkout.

I gained 30 pounds in the first six months of our marriage, so trust me, we never went hungry or felt deprived. Tibby and I worked 40 hours a week and pooled our paychecks. We always knew how much income we had to pay our bills and live on. I used a simple budget on a legal pad each month, never feeling out of control or coming up short to pay our bills.

Today, 51 years later, we remain on a budget but use Quickbooks to maintain complete awareness of every expense and source of income for our personal lives and business obligations, using three joint personal and business checking and savings accounts.

There are several key results learned from our budgeting discipline. By design, Tibby rarely worked outside of the home, maybe a total of three years. This allowed us to prioritize family life even to the present day, because Tibby became heavily involved with the grandkids' lives from birth, as our two daughters and daughter-in-law have joined our Sandler Training and development business.

Fast forward to today, five of the seven grandkids have already graduated from college with their degrees and we remain very close as a family. Along the way to being semi-retired (by choice), we built a northern Pennsylvania mountain home for our growing clan of 15, and recently welcomed our first granddaughter-in-law.

Being disciplined financially through a budget initially allowed me to leave my position as director of training at Preston Trucking (along with its guaranteed salary) in the middle of the 1990 recession while two kids were ready for college and one was not far behind. We made a large investment that we did not have, went to zero income, doubled our monthly expenses, and began with zero customers and only enough savings to last 6-8 months, tops, before we would lose it all. We refer to that decision as "our days of temporary insanity."

We steadily grew the business, purchased, and built our own training center and office in 2005, which is now completely paid for and valued in excess of $400k. During this time, we also experienced a separate business loss of $250k, which we were able to pay off in less than 10 years. At that point in our journey we were in approximately $700k total debt with $250k charged on ten credit cards.

Since then, we have experienced timeshare family vacations, trips to dozens of states and resorts, and over the past 25 years, each were completely paid for through a planned vacation savings account. Today, we are closing in on being completely debt free while owning our house and business condo, free to do whatever we want financially.

Bottom line... if a kid from a low-income, single-parent home with only a 12th-grade education can achieve and experience a life that is financially balanced and fulfilled, so can you.

Never Too Young to Start

Now obviously, Tibby and I are grateful for our lives because of our consistency and discipline for budgeting, but our greatest joys have been to watch our children and grandchildren learn and apply good budgeting principles for themselves and their families. Consequently, each is poised to become financially independent long before we ever did. Of particular joy, we share our 27-year-old grandson's budgeting case study.

As a teenager, Jake asked me to teach him how to budget. And he also framed the Balance Wheel above his bed to remind him of the concepts we talked about.

At age 16, Jake started working at Little Caesar's Pizza for $7.50 per hour. He spent 3-4 years working with autistic young adults for around $10 per hour. For the past 3-4 years he's been working at an assisted-living home specializing in the care of dementia and Alzheimer's residents, averaging $11-13 per hour.

Jake has now earned his Associate's degree in Human Resources over 6-7 years, paying cash as he went, and graduating completely debt-free of any college loans. He plans to live in a double-wide beach house in the eastern U.S. by age 30, when his new car will be completely paid off. He'll use that money for his monthly mortgage and utilities cost.

Jake has currently saved over $15,000 toward his beach house purchase price, despite incurring thousands of dollars in medical expenses this past year.

All this... accomplished in less than 10 years, while averaging $3k-15k annually! Statistically, very few people earning even twice as much or more than Jake come even close to his achievements.

What are Jake's secrets?

- He has a disciplined budget.

- He shops at stores like Dollar General and Goodwill, purchasing name brand, like-new clothing, sneakers, furniture, and household items at 10 to 20% of retail prices.

Proud Grandparent Note: All the financial planning and budgeting advice in the world could not help you more than following Jake's discipline and consistent commitment to living a financially balanced and fulfilling life.

Never Too Old to Start

My single-parent mother was 62 years old when we took her to Disney World. At that time, when I sat down with Mom to discuss her financial situation, we discovered:

- She had an average of $18.35 per month of discretionary income after expenses, while still living alone in our family home of 45 years, with absolutely no savings.

- After I explained Mom's economic reality on paper, she agreed to a plan for her to start budgeting using the envelope method, which she continued into her eighties until my sister took over her daily finances.

- We agreed to sell the family house, which allowed Mom to pay off her debts, buy her first brand new car ever with cash, and deposit $33k in safe mutual funds.

Upon communicating Mom's financial plight to our siblings, all seven of us agreed to send a monthly amount to supplement her Social Security and help cover her house rental payment. After that first year of budgeting, Mom told me it was the first time in her life that she was able to pay all her bills on time.

Special Note: For the next 28 years until Mom passed at age 90, she lived debt-free and accumulated over $22k in her checkbook, plus the invested mutual funds as part of her estate. An extra dividend was that her seven kids got to grow closer than ever and be guilt-free when Mom passed, knowing we had enabled her to live the last third of her life, stress-free of financial burden. I hope you can see how the Balance Wheel areas again affect and impact one another in so many ways.

A Parable

> A man going on a journey entrusted his property to his servants. To one he gave five bags of silver, to another two bags, and to another one bag, each according to his ability.
>
> The man who had received the five bags went at once and put his money to work and gained five more. So also the man with two bags gained two more. But the man who had received the one bag went off, dug a hole in the ground and hid his master's money.
>
> To the first two men the master said, "Well done, good and faithful servant. You have been faithful with a few things. I will put you in charge of many things. Come and share your master's happiness."
>
> But to the one who'd hidden his bag of silver, he said, "You wicked, lazy servant." Then he ordered, "Take the money from him and give it to the one who has the ten bags." [32]

This parable of Jesus is a great example of the butterfly effect. Clearly there are two paths, one to blessing and one to breakdown.

The path to blessing is marked with discipline, consistency, and delayed gratification. Those who walk this path begin with the end in mind. They have a clear picture of what they're shooting for, what they want to accomplish, and what life will look like because of the decisions they're making. They're willing to wait for their reward knowing they are doing the right things. When you choose this path, there are no shortcuts; consistent effort, sacrifice, and discipline are required. But this path gives them the strength to endure

---

[32] Matthew 25:14-28.

obstacles, hardships, challenges, and disappointments to weather any storm, to enjoy a peace that surpasses human understanding.

In stark contrast, the path to breakdown is marked with laziness, compromise, and instant gratification. Those who choose this path make excuses for not doing what they should. They aren't willing to sacrifice or do what's necessary for success because the price is too high and it's too much work. When they don't see the results of their efforts, they give up all too easily. When you choose this path, you compromise your standards by letting your problems and poor decisions accumulate over time until they seem insurmountable. You sacrifice deep, long-term benefit for shallow, short-term pleasure. This group, like most Americans, prioritize how to manage their money in the following order:

a. Spend it (me)
b. Repay debt (me)
c. Pay taxes (government)
d. Save some (me)
e. Give it (others and God)

God is the last on the list and gets the leftovers, yet these same people have no problem begging and blaming God for their financial woes. Obviously, this plan does not work.

Admit—Commit—Submit

- What worldview thinking are you ready to *admit* to that is negatively impacting your financial health?

- What biblical view are you ready to *commit* to pursuing to replace negative and ineffective behaviors that keep you from experiencing financial freedom?

- Who are you prepared to *submit* to for regular accountability regarding your new commitments on taking control of your financial future?

Planning Your Financial Freedom

Success doesn't just happen, you set it in motion. So it is with financial freedom. You will never change where you are until you change what you are doing. Live within the means God is presently providing and budget to correct your spending habits. Make God your partner and practice faith-giving regularly.

Closing Scripture

"Wealth from get-rich-quick schemes quickly disappears; wealth from hard work grows over time." (Proverbs 13:11)

"Riches won't help on the day of judgment, but right living can save you from death." (Proverbs 11:4)

"After all, we brought nothing with us into this world, and we can't take anything with us when we leave." (I Timothy 6:7)

"For the love of money is the root of all kinds of evil. And some people, craving money, have wandered from the true faith and pierced themselves with many sorrows." (I Timothy 6:10)

"Those who love money will never have enough. How meaningless to think that wealth brings true happiness." (Ecclesiastes 5:10)

"No one can serve two masters. For you will hate one and love the other; you will be devoted to one and despise the other. You cannot serve both God and money." (Matthew 6:24)

"Give freely and become more wealthy, be stingy and lose everything." (Proverbs 11:24)

"The generous will prosper; those who refresh others will themselves be refreshed." (Proverbs 11:25)

Closing Prayer

Father, I know little things matter. Even the smallest things I do, think, and say, add up over time. Nudge me to pay attention to the accumulation of my choices. Reveal what I need to change to get on the right path. Give me discipline to consistently do the work in the little things behind the scenes that will lead to life and big, good things.

Help me sacrifice temporary pleasures for long-term satisfaction, all for your glory.

9 | PHYSICAL

Simple answers and practical tips
for physical balance

"Physical training is good, but training for godliness is much better, promising benefits in this life and in the life to come."[33] Throughout our journey, we have reinforced the absolute fact that each life area impacts others dramatically, determining the degree of a balanced or imbalanced life.

Statistically, the overwhelming majority of people are so far out of balance physically, it can't help but impact every area of their lives. Despite billions of dollars spent annually toward quick-fix remedies of dieting, exercise, nutrition, supplements, and sexual conduct, many more billions are spent on medical costs for the damage we bring on ourselves by abusing our physical bodies.

---

[33] I Timothy 4:8.

Once again we can easily discover why these standalone remedies and worldview thinking fail miserably to produce sustained positive results for a healthy and balanced physical life. Our challenge remains the same... look into the mirror and seriously ask yourself, "How badly do you want to be physically fit and balanced?"

Begin by admitting how many of the above quick-fix remedies you have attempted and failed at achieving. How has that affected your sense of self-worth over the years?

Life Detox vs. Detox Diet

Wisdom Walks notes the need to "put off the old to put on the new!" A popular movement in the health and fitness world is the concept of a detox diet. You can hardly pick up a magazine without some reference to detoxing your body to remove the accumulation of harmful substances from the food you eat, the stress you feel, and the environmental toxins you absorb.

Eating a clean diet and taking proper supplements for a period of time can restore a healthy internal environment and promote good health. You'll most likely experience increased energy, reduced aches and pains, better digestion, and fewer illnesses. Capturing and removing toxic substances and replacing them with healthy things are solid life practices. They don't happen automatically without being intentional.

The Bible gives plenty of instructions for detoxifying your life. The Apostle Paul hits it hard when he tells us to "purify ourselves from everything that contaminates body and spirit."[34] Purifying the body includes paying attention to what we eat and drink, staying away from harmful things like

---

34 II Corinthians 7:1.

smoking or drugs, getting proper exercise and enough rest, and not engaging in immoral sexual behavior. Purifying the spirit includes monitoring our words, thoughts, attitudes, actions, and desires.

Clearly, detoxification is not a passive process. We have to act. We put filters on our computers to block viruses, filters on home heating systems to remove dust and allergens, and oil filters on cars to remove debris so the car can perform well and last. But we often don't do much to protect our body, our mind, or our heart.

Life Detox involves three parts.[35] First you must *identify* it. Each of us has harmful stuff in our life that causes damage. Just as your liver is designed to identify harmful substances and capture the toxic material to remove it from your body so it doesn't cause illness, you must identify toxic material in order to remove it from you life. Such content can enter your system in a number of ways, through movies, TV programs, internet sites with inappropriate or offensive material, or music with a great beat but a destructive message. Unhealthy food can also destroy health over time. Dwelling on negative thoughts, having a pattern of critical words, and getting frustrated and angry easily are other detrimental activities than can lead to an unhealthy physical life. No matter what the toxic material, you've got to see it for what it is first.

Second, you have to *remove* it. Once you know the harmful things you're exposing yourself to, you can remove them. Some things just need to go, like a cancerous tumor. Colossians 3 instructs us to remove whatever hinders us from living a life that pleases God. The short list includes anger, slander, foul language, lust, greed, jealousy, lies and

---

[35] From *Wisdom Walks*, by Dan Britton and Jimmy Page.

more. These things poison us; we've got to root them out and get rid of them.

Proverbs 4:23-27 directs us to guard our heart, hold our tongue, keep our eyes from viewing garbage and take the narrow road of obedience. Removing toxic behavior requires you to put up guardrails, draw hard lines you won't cross and get rid of everything that causes you to stumble or fail. You must remove yourself from compromising situations and reduce the opportunity for sin and unhealthy living.

Third, you must *replace* it. It's one thing to stop doing hurtful things, to remove temptations and put up boundaries, but living a holy life requires you to replace the bad with good and replace the don'ts with do's.

Matthew 12:43-45 reveals what happens when we try to clean up all the bad things and neglect to replace them with good. It's like trying to give up sweets without replacing them with a happy, healthy alternative or trying to quit smoking without replacing it with some other better habit. Eventually, the bad habits return with a vengeance.

It's time to put off the "old" and put on the "new." Wrong thinking must be replaced with right thinking—the possible and the pure. Criticism must be replaced with encouragement. Anger must be replaced with love and tenderness. A life detox is a perfect way to purify yourself from everything that contaminates your mind, body, and spirit.

"Because we have these promises, dear friends, let us cleanse ourselves from everything that can defile our body or spirit. And let us work toward complete holiness because we fear God."[36]

---

[36] II Corinthians 7:1.

Much of the motivation promoted by society or worldview advice regarding your physical improvement is to focus on how you will look on the outside, and how that new look, including your hair color, will prove that you are worth it. Just like all the other advice, thinking and marketing for how to have it all for the other areas of your life wheel is to focus on Me, Me, Me!. In contrast, the biblical motivation found in I Corinthians 3:16 challenges us: "Don't you realize that all of you together are the temple of God and that the Spirit of God lives in you?"

I Corinthians 6:19-20 goes deeper. "You do not belong to yourself, for God bought you with a high price. So you must honor God with your body."

God's reminder centers around the fact that he created you, loves you, and proved that love by sacrificing his Son's life on a cross for everyone who will accept Jesus Christ as their Savior and make him Lord of their entire lives. The critical decision of who is in control of your life—yourself or God—will ultimately determine how good you will look and feel physically about yourself, both on the inside and outside.

Simple, Practical, Effective Advice for Physical Health

Regardless of your age or gender, you can develop and sustain healthy eating and exercise habits throughout your lifetime. Balanced life winners practice preventive maintenance, both professionally and personally.

During my 20 years in sales and management with two of the nation's largest trucking companies, I was exposed to practical and effective tools for improving productivity.

1. PIP—Performance Improvement Process
2. PMP—Preventive Maintenance Programs

I learned that winning organizations create a culture of excellence which forces leadership to think differently, especially in the areas of investment versus cost.

The motto of non-winners and mediocre companies and individuals is: "If it ain't broke, don't fix it," always viewing expenses as controlling short-term costs. However, winning organizations and individuals understand that assets, whether equipment or personnel, require regular, ongoing, gradual, and incremental investments to ensure greater long-term ROI as well as ROE, a return on both investment and energy.

Subsequently, I witnessed millions of dollars invested in regular preventive maintenance on thousands of tractors, trailers, and forklifts. At Preston Trucking we saved tens of millions over the long haul in the areas of equipment longevity, gas mileage, fewer breakdowns, and other key performance indicators.

Since I was privileged to work for a visionary CEO, he saw something extra in me. Along with his vision to create a university of training for sales and management and team development similar to Disney and 3M Universities, he asked me to create and conduct Preston University as the company's director of training.

At age 35, I found my niche in life as I witnessed significant growth in all those who embraced change and accepted 100% responsibility for their individual growth, regardless of sex, age, color, or background. I was also struck by the biblical principle found in the book of Proverbs that notes that untrained apprentices with a proper attitude will outperform skilled veterans with wrong attitudes every single time!

Applying the PIP and PMP improvement principles with humans for nearly five years resulted in many changed lives and tens of millions of dollars in increased sales and productivity improvements. Those concepts became the strong motivations for me to voluntarily leave the security of my corporate management position to become an entrepreneur and sole proprietor of a Sandler Sales and Personal Development franchise at age 40, with no financial backing. Thirty-one years later, my family and I still challenge businesses and individuals to think differently and commit to a lifetime of ongoing, gradual, and incremental development.

So for those who say, "If it ain't broke, don't fix it," let me ask you this question. How is that working for you personally regarding your physical health? How much are you spending on medical costs, high insurance premiums, uncovered procedures, and various quick-fix remedies in an attempt to improve your physical health in hopes of looking like someone on a magazine cover?

In the end, no one is happy with the large cost to repair or replace houses, cars, air conditioners, heaters, lawn mowers, and other machines. Yet the body is God's created machine for us, and he and his word encourage us to honor him by taking good care of that body, which allows us to enjoy longer lasting benefits and quality of life. We spend billions in insurance to help cover repair and replacement costs, that in many cases, preventive maintenance measures would have helped us avoid.

Another option is that we could respect our bodies by remembering health is life's first prize. Many will spend our health gaining wealth, then gladly pay all we have earned to get our health back. An effective act of prevention is to be good to your body by giving it the sleep, the surroundings, the exercise, and the proper food and nutrition it deserves because it's the only machine God will allow you to inhabit during this lifetime. You need to value it!

Practical Advice

To help me reach younger generations, I requested the assistance of another of my special grandchildren, Abby Kaufman, not only because her brother Jacob was the case study in the Financial chapter, but because Abby epitomizes what it means to physically be "all in" at developing and sustaining a beautiful life of balance.

Before you consider discounting Abby's qualifications to speak as an expert on how to live a balanced life because of her age, you may want to visit YouTube and search for "Abby Kaufman gymnast," especially if you have young daughters with aspirations of pursuing gymnastics.

Abby, started gymnastics at age two. She spent 19 years in a club gym and university gym, including four years on a full-ride gymnastics scholarship at West Virginia University, averaging over 20 hours per week.

Some of her accomplishments include:

- 5-time Pennsylvania All-Around State Champion
- Level 10 N.I.T. National All-Around Champion
- Highest single-season point total in WVU history for 14 All-Around events
- 2019 Big 12 Scholar Athlete of the Year
- Eight years of cyber school with a 4.0 GPA
- 3.97 GPA for four years at WVU
- Proud member of the Fellowship of Christian Athletes

- Recipient of West Virginia University's most prestigious Order of Augusta, recognizing superior scholarship, demonstrated leadership and record of community and public service.

All these achievements and more were accomplished despite numerous body changes, injuries, and stresses at the highest levels of an academic and athletic Division I competitive environment. None of us may ever aspire to a journey similar to Abby's, but she has much to share that can help you achieve improved physical health and a high degree of life balance.

Since graduating with her four-year degree and presently pursuing her Physician's Assistant degree back at WVU, Abby became a Beachbody On-Demand Life Coach.[37] She generously shares the following advice to encourage you to your own improved health and life balance.

Build Healthy Eating Habits and Make Them Stick

At the start of your health and fitness journey, let go of the urge to find and follow the perfect diet to a tee. Keep in mind that setbacks are normal and learning to deal with them is critical for making healthy eating habits stick.

Why eat healthy? Can you overdo healthy eating?

First, you need to make a healthy eating plan. This includes choosing mostly whole, unprocessed foods. Plan ahead when you shop for food. When you sit down to eat, mind your portions. Develop and maintain a balanced, healthy-ish mindset, and above all... celebrate your wins!

What prevents you from eating healthy?

---

[37] Read more from Abby at:
https://www.beachbodyondemand.com/blogs

Various components contribute, including not having social support, a lack of time, feeling deprived, and losing motivation too early.

To get your day started right, here are some helpful breakfast tips:

- Keep it simple. No need for fancy recipes. Try a banana, peanut butter, apples, toast, or eggs.

- Decide what you're going to have for breakfast the night before, and set an alarm.

- Do meal prep on Sundays—egg muffin cups, overnight oats, etc.

- Wake up 10 minutes early, and make that extra awake time worth it!

- Have a glass of water ready on the counter for when you wake up.

Five Surprising Benefits of Exercise You Haven't Considered

1. Exercise may help alleviate depression and anxiety.

2. Exercise helps you poop.

3. Exercise helps you relax and get some Z's.

4. Exercise helps you be more productive.

5. Exercise helps boost your self-esteem.

Why Your Daily Workout Isn't Working

There are several possibilities for why your daily workout no longer gives the benefits you are seeking. Perhaps you don't have a clear goal or are not challenging yourself enough.

Boredom with your workout is a leading reason for decreased effectiveness.

If you do the exact same thing every day it will cease to provide the same level of workout. Also check in to make sure you are practicing with proper form.

Remember to get enough sleep and give yourself plenty of time to recover. In addition to replenishing these physical resources, make sure you eat enough total calories of the right proportions, including protein, and stay properly hydrated.

You might wake up feeling like you're moving at the pace of a sloth. Every day you will not be 100% of your max performance. What matters is that you put in 100% effort despite how you feel. That's when you get better and grow stronger.

You can do this.

How to Bounce Back and Get On Track

Falling off the wagon happens to everyone, even if you set exciting goals. Regardless of why you've lost sight of your goals, being hard on yourself is not the way forward.

"Giving up on your goals because of one setback is like slashing your other three tires because you got one flat."

Here are some strategies for getting back on track and starting healthy habits:

1. Be specific
2. Have a plan

3. Be mindful
4. Don't do it because you should
5. Be your own best friend
6. Let go of the all-or-nothing attitude
7. Remove known hurdles
8. Check in with yourself and others

You will never, always be motivated, so you must learn to be disciplined.

For a Happy and Healthy Life

1. Wake up earlier
2. Ditch the scarcity mindset
3. Invest in yourself
4. Test your limits
5. Protect your skin
6. Eat mindfully
7. Stay active
8. Make gut health a priority
9. Cook your own meals
10. Drink more water
11. Stay inspired
12. Take action
13. Be accountable

Truth Bomb

Everything in life is about priorities, and what you prioritize will dictate what your life looks like. Here's a list of choices many people make, and the mindset that holds them back.

$100 dinner date...	seems reasonable
but $100 healthy groceries...	too expensive!
$100 night out drinking...	weekly occurrence
but $100 supplements...	can't afford that!
$250 Gucci belt...	gotta have it
but $250 personal growth seminar...	that's crazy talk!
$1000 iPhone	need the newest
but $1000 to start a business...	I can't justify that
60 min. watching Netflix...	time flies
60 min. at the gym...	wish I had the time

The Hacks

Success is all about priorities, and balanced people prioritize investing in themselves. What are your "why's" for achieving a healthy physical life?

Your "why" must be personal. It can be temporary, and it will definitely evolve over time.

Your "why" should help you focus on your goal. It fuels your discipline and helps you to be resilient.

Your "why" can be quite simple. Its power is that it melts your fears.

Your "why" doesn't have to please anyone else. Your "why" is yours and yours alone.

Visualize the Attainment of Your Dreams

Your mind is an incubator that gives birth to ideas and dreams. What you concentrate on, you will feel. What you feel, you will eventually perform. What you perform, you will become. What you become determines your destiny.

What you see in your mind will happen in time. So see yourself victorious, healthy, and blessed!

Admit—Commit—Submit

- What worldview thinking are you ready to *admit* to that is negatively impacting your physical health balance?

- What biblical view are you ready to *commit* to pursuing to replace negative and ineffective ways of caring for your physical condition?

- Who are you prepared to *submit* to for regular accountability regarding your new commitments to improving your physical well-being?

*"Good timber does not grow with ease;
the stronger the wind, the stronger the trees."*
—*J. Willard Marriott, Adversity Quotient*

Closing Scripture

"Physical training is good, but training for godliness is much better, promising benefits in this life and in the life to come." (I Timothy 4:8)

"Don't you realize that all of you together are the temple of God and that the Spirit of God lives in you? God will destroy anyone who destroys this temple. For God's temple is holy, and you are that temple." (I Corinthians 3:16-17)

"Run from sexual sin! No other sin so clearly affects the body as this one does. For sexual immorality is a sin against your own body. Don't you realize that your body is the temple of the Holy Spirit, who lives in you and was given to you by God? You do not belong to yourself, for God bought you with a high price. So you must honor God with your body." (I Corinthians 6:18-20)

Live Intentionally and Maximize Your Efforts

Spend time with God in prayer. Ask God to reveal to you any toxic behaviors you're not already aware of. Write down everything he tells you in a journal. Confess any wrongdoing and sinful behavior and ask him to forgive you. Ask him to give you the courage and determination to change what needs to be changed.

Closing Prayer

Father, I know it's time to take action and purify my life from everything that contaminates me. I also know it's time to pursue a holy life out of reverence for you. I want my life to be different. Please help me to make decisions that lead to life. Cleanse me of my sin and set me free from its burden. Help me find specific ways to replace the old with the new and to walk in good health—mind, body, and spirit.

10 | FAMILY

Marriage & Children—blessing or curse

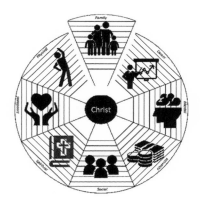

"Children are a gift from the Lord; they are a reward from him. Children born to a young man are like arrows in a warrior's hands. How joyful is the man whose quiver is full of them! He will not be put to shame when he confronts his accusers at the city gates." (Psalm 127:3-5)

I have purposely saved our conversation on family, knowing that you will be able to relate to real-life experiences, and how they have impacted every other area of your life, regardless of your current and past family situations.

No other area of life is being challenged and debated more due to the conflict between worldview and biblical thinking, except our spiritual beliefs, which we will discuss in the next chapter.

So what constitutes a family?

As written in Genesis 2:18-25, the Lord said it isn't good for man to be alone. He made a woman and brought her to the man. For that reason, a man will leave his father and mother and be united to his wife. This text is used to illustrate God's wrath against mankind's worldview of same-sex unions.

Romans 1:24-27 says: "God abandoned them to do whatever shameful things their hearts desired. As a result, they did vile and degrading things with each other's bodies. They traded the truth about God for a lie. So they worshiped and served the things God created instead of the Creator himself, who is worthy of eternal praise! Amen. That is why God abandoned them to their shameful desires. Even the women turned against the natural way to have sex and instead indulged in sex with each other. And the men, instead of having normal sexual relations with women, burned with lust for each other. Men did shameful things with other men, and as a result of this sin, they suffered within themselves the penalty they deserved."

Now, before you want to burn this book and its writer, I encourage you to consider that you have already read nine chapters, which demonstrated the positive and negative consequences for placing your own thinking at the center of your Balance Wheel instead of God. So regardless of your like or dislike of God's position on marriage and family, let's look at the brutal facts as we view the statistical, emotional, physical, social, financial, and career consequences that continue to plague humanity and its worldview thinking.

As someone who came from divorced parents, raised with six siblings by a single mother, and after being the husband of one woman for over 51 years and father of three adult married children with seven young-adult grandchildren, my intent is not to bring additional pain to anyone who has suffered as a child of divorce, or in a single-parent household or as a member of a stepfamily. I take zero pleasure in the following staggering statistics, but I share them with the intent to help confront the growing insane thinking which leads to so much pain, imbalance, and a lack of hope for the future.

The majority of family types has shifted from a biologically bonded mother–father–child. We are now a nation and a world in which the majority of families are divorced. Most go on to remarry or form living-together relationships. These families take a multitude of forms:

- Divorced with children. The children reside with one parent and visit the other; most are dating, looking for new partners

- Remarried, re-coupled, living together with his and/or her children. He/she is in the role of step-parent

- Single mothers, recoupling, dating and alone

- Divorced dads. These dads generally visit their children, often they are recoupled, bringing a stepmother figure into their children's lives

- Lesbian and gay couples with children from a prior relationship

The U.S. Bureau of Census relates that 1300 new stepfamilies are forming every day. Over 50% of U.S. families are remarried or recoupled. The average marriage in America lasts only seven years, and one out of two marriages ends in divorce. Around 75% of those divorced people remarry, and 66% of those living together or remarried wind up breaking up when children are involved.

For nearly 80% of those remarried or coupled partners who have children, both have careers. Of the 60 million children under the age of 13, 50% currently live with one biological parent and that parent's partner.

A Boston University psychologist researcher reported that of the career women who earn over $100k and who married men with children from a previous relationship, over 75% said that if they had to do it again, they would not make the same choice. Finally, 50% of all women—not just mothers—are likely sometime in their life to live in a stepfamily relationship (this includes living-together families).[38]

Children of Divorce

Judith Wallerstein is a psychologist and author of *Second Chances and the Unexpected Legacy of Divorce*. Wallerstein reports that only 45% of children do well after divorce. Another 41% are doing poorly, worried, underachieving, and are often angry. The anger doesn't stop with the children. Around 50% of the women and 30% of the men were still intensely angry with their former spouses.

Most children of divorce felt the lack of a template, a working model, for a loving relationship between a man and a woman. Their divorced parents spent less time with them, established households with less discipline, and were less sensitive to the children's needs due to issues surrounding their own divorce and its aftermath.

Wallerstein reports that many parents are unable to separate their needs from the children's needs and often share too much of their personal life, placing the children in a

[38] Research compiled by Professor of Sociology Larry L. Burnpass of the University of Wisconsin.

precarious emotional state, vulnerable to grandiosity or to depression within what is left of their families.

The majority of children of divorce who later become parents are chronically disorganized and unable to parent effectively. As diminished parenting continues, it permanently disrupts the child's once normal emotional growth and functioning.

Elizabeth Marquart is a scholar with the Institute for American Values, a think tank on family issues. Her study shows that children often grow up torn between two households. Bodies of research are emerging on at least two sides of the debate. Marquart is among those who believe that even under the best of circumstances, children suffer emotional scars that last a lifetime and have trouble with their own intimate relationships as adults.

Marquart hates the term *the good divorce.* "Just because parents don't continue to argue doesn't mean the kids do well." She says that *good divorce* is an "adult-centered vision." No matter the level of conflict, a divided family often requires children to confront a whole set of challenges that children in intact families do not have to face. Her major conclusion is that children of divorce must go from living in one world that seems safe to going back and forth between two homes that often feel like "polar opposites."

The kids must perform higher level tasks that parents would normally provide—develop a clear view of what to think, what to believe, and how to behave... especially in the moral and spiritual realms. It becomes the child's job to synthesize these two worlds.

Marquart conducted a national survey of 1500 young adults, now aged 18 to 35. About half are from divorced families and half from intact families. Those from divorced families were younger than age 14 when the split occurred. She also interviewed 71 young adults to probe their inner feelings. She says children of divorced parents are more apt than those living in intact families to feel divided between two homes with different values. They are asked to keep secrets about the different households. They are left without clear guidance of what is right and what is wrong, turning instead to friends and siblings, and they are more apt to struggle with loss, isolation, loneliness and suffering.

Wallerstein applauds Marquart. "Her observations are right on target," Wallerstein says. "These children have a sense of living in two different worlds. They grow up with difficulty in feeling whole."

Single-Parent Households

Single parents are everywhere in today's society. They are church members, coworkers, leaders, daughters, mothers, fathers and grandparents. But the numbers are staggering:

- 86% of single-parent families in the U.S. are led by mothers. Also 57% of millennial mothers are single moms.

- In 2017, 25% of U.S. households were headed by a single parent.

Talking about single-parenthood would be incomplete without talking about the children, the most fragile partakers of single-parenthood. As shown below, the number of children in single-parent households is increasing, consistent with the growing number of solo parents.

- As of 2019, there were 15.76 million children living with their single mothers in the U.S.

- In the same year, 3.23 million children were living with their single fathers.

- In 2019, 21k children under the age of one lived with their divorced single father.

- In 2017, 21% of children under 18 years old were living with single moms, whereas 4% were with single dads.

Mental Health Struggle

Worryingly, 20.6% of moms who were single at childbirth experienced postpartum depression. In addition, 11.5% of young mothers who were cohabitating at childbirth experienced postpartum depression. In another study, scientists found that single mothers had massively higher odds of suffering from mood disorders than married mothers.

The struggles that single parents face are as clear as day. However, the magnitude and impact of these challenges differ uniquely, depending on how the parent ended up going it alone. For example, those who are in it as a result of bereavement may have an entirely different financial situation compared to the divorced. A single mom with three children can have a far steeper mountain to climb than a solo parent with one child.

Raising children alone isn't a situation many parents choose or wish to be in. Many times, however, fate decides otherwise, forcing parents to run the race alone. With the cost of raising children shooting upwards, and earning power declining, the odds are stacked against single parents. In the midst of all the struggle, poverty has sharpened its claws, waiting to pounce on those who gave up too soon.

Why is single-parenthood on the rise? Data shows that the skyrocketing number of single moms and dads is the result of many driving factors. Key among them is a decreasing, yet still high, divorce rate and a downhill trend for marriage rates. Of course, the overall acceptance of same-sex marriage among young people has played a part in pushing the rates of single-parenthood through the roof.

Decreasing Marriage Rates

The values of the traditional family settings have been diluted and this has been marked by an increase in nontraditional families. Today, marriage is regarded by many as an obsolete institution that often doesn't preclude romantic relationships. The result? Well, the falling single-parent statistics also paint the dull image of the declining marriage rates.

- The number of marriages in the U.S. decreased by 103,643 between 2017 and 2018.

- The support for legalization of same-sex marriage has contributed to increasing rates of single motherhood. In 2017, 62% of Americans supported the legalization of same-sex marriage.

It's clear that when marriage is impeded or broken, single-parenthood is born. Beyond this, the shift in social values and norms, coupled with a reduction in the stigma associated with nonmarital childbearing and divorce, has massively contributed to the growing case of single-parenthood.

The above data has missed an intriguing point, and we cannot afford to let it go untouched. Individualism has encouraged people, especially the younger generations, to put personal gratification above family responsibility. In some cases, people develop a tendency to ask far more than they get from their marriages, and when expectations aren't met, marriages go sour.

Challenges of Single-parent Households

Nearly all cases of single-parenthood are best defined as bittersweet love stories. Often the journey began in the shape of a romantic relationship that ended in a bitter breakup. When marriages are involved, these tussles often head to the corridors of justice in the form of custody battles. And in other cases, love birds may have bitter breakups even before they walk down the aisle.

In all cases, it's a bare fact that one parent is left to shoulder all the responsibilities of bringing up the "fruits" of their broken relationship. Doing it alone isn't a piece of cake. It's a tough journey that bombards the solo parent with all sorts of challenges, key among them being financial problems.

The lack of money causes anxiety for the population in general, but especially single parents. Running a households, raising children and juggling between financial commitments are monstrous duties for solo parents. And, as shown by the following single-parent statistics, many have crumbled under the pressure and are now languishing in poverty, unable to provide basic food and shelter.

- 44% of single mothers in the world struggled to afford food in 2019.

- In the United States, 40% of single moms have trouble affording food, whereas 27% struggle to afford shelter.

- Countries with the highest rate of single moms who couldn't afford shelter in 2019 included Lithuania at

36%, Estonia at 36%, France at 30%, and the U.S. at 27%.

- 65% of single moms in sub-Saharan African countries struggled to put food on the table in 2019.

Saddening Statistics for 2021[39]

There is no denying that going through a divorce can impact many different people. Sure, it has an obvious impact on the couple who has decided to part ways, but it also affects their family and friends. Children are the most likely to go through a parent's divorce struggling mightily.

With that in mind, the eye-opening statistics for children of divorce help us comprehend the overall impact of this traumatic life event.

But before digging deep into each stat, let's have a quick look at what divorce does to a child.

One-third of all marriages in the U.S. end in divorce, the third-highest divorce rate in the world. Of those, 73% report they get divorced because of a lack of commitment. From the remaining couples, half get divorced because they argued too much and the other half because of cheating.

Apart from the primary reason, 46% of divorced people say they got divorced because they married too young, 45% had unrealistic expectations, and 44% felt the partnership was not equal. Sadly, 25% were in an abusive relationship.

About 50% of all American children will witness the end of their parents' marriage. Almost half will go on to see a parent's second marriage break up. Moreover, one in every 10 children with divorced parents will then see the breakup

---

39 Marija Lazic, February 25, 2021. "Legal Jobs" blog.

of three or more parental marriages. And more than 20% of children in the U.S. are being raised without their fathers.

According to research carried out in the University College of London, if parents divorce when a child is 7-14 years old, they are likely to experience behavioral issues. Children of divorced parents are twice as likely to drop out of school, according to research from Harvard University Press. This indicates a need to pay special attention to a child's academic performance. If you are going through a divorce, it may even be worth talking to the child's teacher to explain the situation at home.

Another academic side-effect is that teenagers may drop out of school so they can get a job and help their family to pay for rent and food. Children who are young when their parents separate are twice as likely to drop out of school, and have a fear of commitment and a low-paying job. Children who have been through a number of different divorces with their parents usually have lower grade scores when compared with children who have not experienced divorce in the home.

Children of divorced parents are also more likely to get cancer. A reason for this is that they are more likely to participate in activities such as drinking too much alcohol, smoking, and having unprotected sex. These are all activities that have been shown to heighten the risks associated with developing cancer.

Disturbingly, children of divorced parents are twice as likely to attempt suicide. This is one of the most worrying side-effects. Now, this does not mean that you should stay with someone you no longer love, but you do need to pay special attention to how your child is behaving. It can be beneficial for children of divorce to see a therapist during this difficult period to help them understand the situation and talk to someone who is not directly involved in the marriage breakdown.

Children of divorced parents are four times as likely to have social problems. They tend to have more difficulty with peers. When children are frustrated, confused, or unhappy with the situation at home, they can act out and take it out on their friends. They may even feel resentment towards children whose parents are still together.

It is unsurprising to learn that 70% of prison inmates serving long-term sentences grew up in a broken home.

Teenagers of divorced parents are 300% more likely to experience mental health issues. There is also an increased risk of physical health problems, as well as behavioral issues. In fact, teenagers with divorced parents are a lot more likely to experience mental health problems that will require medication, counseling, or both.

Other U.S. Divorce Statistics Related to Children

- Children living with both biological parents are 35% healthier than children of divorced parents. Moreover, children are 50% more likely to become seriously ill after experiencing a parent's divorce.

- Kids from broken homes tend to experience more speech issues as well as headaches, asthma, chronic illness, and injuries.

- Children of divorce are five times more likely to live in poverty, making ends meet on a single income.

So there you have it... these astonishing statistics really drive home the impact divorce can have on a child. You may be shocked to have learned about the sheer number of children who live in broken homes today, but the stats don't lie.

As a parent, you may be able to take some comfort in the knowledge that you are not alone. While it can be difficult, it is vital to make sure that the issues of a divorce do not end up causing problems for your child. There is a lot of help available for you to get the support and assistance you require.

Since the title and purpose of this book is to provide a frame of reference for determining what constitutes a life of balance versus imbalance, these statistics and realities should shock anyone's worldview, but especially those with an I-centered unbiblical position on marriage and family.

Some may falsely believe that having large amounts of money provides immunity from emotional suffering for spouses and children of broken marriages and families. However, consider Bill and Melinda Gates' 2021 announcement that they were ending their 27-year marriage. Their reported $130B net worth and admirable social contributions through their foundation will not compensate for the suffering of their three children.

A Better Way

The choice is yours. By God's grace, I humbly end this chapter that has been filled with dismal but factual information by providing tidbits from my 51-year marriage and family journey.

As the third of seven kids, I was raised with my six siblings by a single mother after a drunk and abusive father left when I was in seventh grade. Even before Dad left, I vividly recall walking to school in sixth grade, visualizing and praying for the type of wife and family I wanted for my future—

specifically one based on harmony and where I vowed never to lay a hand of violence on my wife so I would not repeat the sins of my father.

To my great delight, God not only answered my prayer, but far exceeded my expectations for a godly wife when he gave me Tibby as my life partner.

> *"The man who finds a wife, finds a treasure and receives favor from the Lord." (Proverbs 18:22)*

We were married just before my 20th birthday, motivated by the following goals and vows:

- To be married for 75 years

- To create a 75th anniversary picture of Tibby and me with our extended tribe of kids, grandkids, and great grandkids

- To constantly improve our marriage and parenting skills

- Divorce would never be an option

Tibby and I celebrated our 51st anniversary on September 12, 2021, and our tribe family (see Figure 10.1) now includes 16 members:

- 3 children: Bob, 50; Kelly, 48; and Kate, 42

- Their spouses and 7 grandkids: Jacob, 27; Morgan, 24; Peyton, 23; Trevor, 20; Abby, 22; Alex, 19; and Tyler, 18; along with Trevor's beautiful bride, Kenzie, our first granddaughter-in-law.

Figure 3:(left to right) Front row: C.J., Kate, Jeremy, Kelly, MaryBeth, and Bob. Second row: Ed and Tibby. Third row: Peyton, Alex, Abby, Jacob, Morgan, Kenzie, Trevor, and Tyler.

We have kept our vows and commitments, motivated to never break trust with each other or give our kids and friends any reason to quit and give up on God's plan for all marriages, which is clearly stated in Malachi 2:14-16: "You cry out, 'Why doesn't the Lord accept my worship?' I'll tell you why! Because the Lord witnessed the vows you and your wife made when you were young. But you have been unfaithful to her, though she remained your faithful partner, the wife of your marriage vows. Didn't the Lord make you one with your wife? In body and spirit you are his. And what does he want? Godly children from your union. So guard your heart; remain loyal to the wife of your youth. 'For I hate divorce!' says the Lord, the God of Israel. 'To divorce your wife is to overwhelm her with cruelty,' says the Lord of

Heaven's Armies. 'So guard your heart; do not be unfaithful to your wife'."

I Corinthians 7:10-11 says: "But for those who are married, I have a command that comes not from me, but from the Lord. A wife must not leave her husband. But if she does leave him, let her remain single or else be reconciled to him. And the husband must not leave his wife."

I realize all the pushback to God's plan, but assure everyone who chooses to follow this plan that future marriage and family life can be filled with love, harmony, and incredible fulfillment, compared to all the angst, sorrow, and pain that we covered above as consequences of divorce.

Admit—Commit—Submit

- What worldview are you ready to *admit* to that is negatively impacting your marriage and family?

- What biblical view are you ready to *commit* to pursuing to replace negative and ineffective ways of thinking regarding your marriage and family?

- Who are you prepared to *submit* to for regular accountability regarding your commitment to restoring balance and health to your marriage and family?

Knowledge is not power unless it is properly applied. Knowledge has true value under only three conditions:

1. If it involves worthy matters—marriage and family

2. If it is held by people of worthy character

3. If it is used in a worthy manner—lifelong commitment

Closing Scripture

"The man who finds a wife, finds a treasure, and he receives favor from the Lord." (Proverbs 18:22)

"So a church leader must be a man whose life is above reproach. He must be faithful to his wife. He must exercise self-control, live wisely, and have a good reputation. He must enjoy having guests in his home, and he must be able to teach. He must not be a heavy drinker or be violent. He must be gentle, not quarrelsome, and not love money. He must manage his own family well, having children who respect and obey him. For if a man cannot manage his own household, how can he take care of God's church?" (I Timothy 3:2-5)

"He was a devout, God-fearing man, as was everyone in his household. He gave generously to the poor and prayed regularly to God." (Acts 10:2)

"But if she [a widow] has children or grandchildren, their first responsibility is to show godliness at home and repay their parents by taking care of them. This is something that pleases God." (I Timothy 5:4)

"But those who won't care for their relatives, especially those in their own household, have denied the true faith. Such people are worse than unbelievers." (I Timothy 5:8)

"Greed brings grief to the whole family, but those who hate bribes will live." (Proverbs 15:27)

"She gets up before dawn to prepare breakfast for her household." (Proverbs 31:15)

"Jesus said, 'No, go home to your family, and tell them everything the Lord has done for you and how merciful he has been'." (Mark 5:19)

Closing Thought

New thinking leads to starting a new generation. Throughout our *Life of Balance vs. Imbalance* journey, I have unashamedly attributed the number one contributing factor for a balanced life to be determined by our choice of who we will give control of every area of our lives. Hang in there as we challenge you with how your Spiritual aspects impact your entire quality of life.

11 | SPIRITUAL

"Trusted relationship for living" vs. "Religion"

"Lord, we don't know where you are going, so how can we know the way?" Jesus answered, "I am the way and the truth and the life. No one comes to the Father except through me." (John 14:1-6, NIV)

One Way

The path you pick leads to life or death. From the very beginning, and throughout our entire *Life of Balance vs. Imbalance* journey, I have unashamedly asserted that the *ultimate answer* to which life we all are traveling on is determined by our individual decision of *who* we place at the center of our Balance Wheel—ourselves or Jesus Christ.

I have consistently reminded you of Christ's words that tell us that as a man or woman thinks, that's what leads to their behavior or life actions.[40] Consequently, each chapter challenged you, the reader, to choose between worldview thinking versus biblical thinking, supported with numerous scriptures from the word of God.

In this chapter, I will do my very best to challenge you to compare your thinking to what God says instead of what the world says, since what we admit, commit and submit to determines the quality of our lives, not only here on Earth, but ultimately where we will spend eternity.

As a reminder, I am not a pastor or Bible scholar, but I am someone who became a believer and follower of Christ 40 years ago and has read, studied, and taught the Bible cover-to-cover for the past 34 years, choosing to allow God to direct my thoughts, words, and deeds as his child and as a husband, father, grandfather, friend, professional life coach, and business owner. It remains my hope and goal to provide you, the reader, with the answers and solutions for any areas of imbalance in your life where you feel hopeless to address and resolve them.

In Jeremiah 29:11, for everyone who chooses God's intended life path he promises: "For I know the plans I have for you," declares the Lord. "Plans for welfare and not for evil, to give you a future and a hope."

Everyone wants to know the right path to choose, but usually we're already convinced we're going the right way. However, Proverbs 14:12 says that in the end, what we think is the right way leads to death.

Many philosophies and religions prescribe a list of all the things you need to do to go to heaven. In this age of tolerance and relative truth, you may hear a common phrase that, "All

---

[40] Proverbs 23:7, *NKJV*.

roads lead to heaven." You may also hear, "Whatever works for you." But that isn't what Jesus teaches.

Jesus says that only one road leads to eternal life, to the Father's house. Jesus is the way, the truth, and the life, and no one comes to the father except through him. He didn't say "a" way; he said "the" way. He was reminding us to follow him. It was the exact thing he'd said when he first called the apostles to follow him, wherever he went, to follow in his footsteps, to do the things they saw him do, to be the kind of person they saw him being.

In John 3:36 (*NIV*) we're told: "Whoever believes in the Son has eternal life, but whoever rejects the Son will not see life." In I Timothy 2:5-6, we're told that Jesus is the one and only "mediator" between God and man. Jesus stands in the gap, arms stretched wide across the cross, so that everyone who believes in him can have their relationship with God restored. He alone can make the connection possible. Not Muhammad, Buddha, Joseph Smith, Hinduism, nor our own efforts and good deeds can make the connection possible.

So what do you believe? Is Jesus really "the" way? You decide. Pick a path. If you choose Jesus, you're compelled to follow him and that implies taking action... putting aside your desires in order to walk his way. But his way always leads to life—eternal life.[41]

Why Believe the Bible?
Evidence for God and His Word

We should believe the Bible because it is the Word of God. There is no other book in the world like the Bible. It is the only book authorized by God as his direct revelation to man.

---

[41] Drawn from *Wisdom Walks* by Dan Britton and Jimmy Page.

The Bible consists of 66 books written over 15 centuries by nearly 40 different writers. Yet it does not contradict itself. Holy men were inspired by the Holy Spirit to write the Holy Scriptures.

"Your word is a lamp to guide my feet and a light for my path." (Psalm 119:105)

Many textbooks become outdated within 10 years, but the Word of God remains up to date. It is new every morning. The Bible is flawlessly accurate. For example, the Old Testament contains numerous predictions about Jesus that were fulfilled in exact detail in the New Testament.

The Bible is also a masterpiece in literature. It has long been the best-selling book in the world. No event in history is better documented than the resurrection of Jesus Christ as recorded in the Scriptures. Christ's resurrection is verified both by historical records and by its effects on the lives of eyewitnesses.

Another way the Bible confirms God's existence is by its fulfilled prophecies. Only God can accurately predict the future, and Bible prophecy has been defined as God's writing history in advance. More than 300 Old Testament prophecies were fulfilled in the life of Christ. The accuracy of the Bible has also been verified repeatedly from archaeology. Without a doubt, the Bible is a supernatural book inspired by the living God.

The Bible has stood the test of all ages. Scoffers have tried for centuries to destroy or disprove the Bible, but they have never succeeded. It transforms people, as Psalm 19:1 (*NIV*) says: "The law of the Lord is perfect, refreshing the soul."

How does the Bible affect us? Do we spend much time reading it? Have we allowed the word of God to grip our heart and change our behavior? We must love it, learn from it, and live by it, for someday we will be judged by the word of God.

> *"God uses it to prepare and equip his people to do every good work."*
> *(II Timothy 3:17)*

There are four simple reasons you need the Bible:

1. *To help you know God.* Nature shows us how God is powerful, creative, and organized and how he likes variety. But God reveals many other things about himself through the Bible to know what God is like. We need the Bible.

2. *To teach you the truth.* In this age of truth decay, who are you going to trust? Politicians? Twitter? The media? Jesus says: "You will know the truth and the truth will set you free."[42] When God speaks through the Bible, he offers eternal truth that you can count on.

3. *To show you how to live.* The Bible is God's big instruction book. It includes the guidance you need to make life work.

4. *To give you spiritual strength.* God will always give you the power to do what he asks. You'll find that power in the spiritual truth of his Word. You never know what the day will bring. Whatever it is, make

---

[42] John 8:32.

sure you're equipped with the Bible, God's owner manual for your life.

God's Goal: Your Character, Not Your Comfort

Many religions and philosophies promote the old lie that humans are divine or can become gods. Let me be absolutely clear—you will never become God or even a god. That prideful lie is Satan's oldest temptation. Satan promised Adam and Eve that if they followed his advice, they would be as gods.[43] This desire to be a god shows up every time you try to control your circumstances, your future, and the people around you. You're a creature; you will never be the Creator.

God doesn't want you to become a god. He wants you to become godly. He wants you to develop his values, attitudes, and character. You are meant to take on an entirely new way of life, a God-fashioned life, a life renewed from the inside and working itself into your conduct as God accurately reproduces his character in you.[44]

God's ultimate goal for your life on Earth is not comfort, but character development. He wants you to grow spiritually and become like Christ. Becoming like Christ does not mean losing your personality or becoming a mindless clone. God created your uniqueness, so he certainly doesn't want to destroy it. Christ likeness is all about transforming your character, not your personality.

God wants you to develop the kind of character described in the Beatitudes of Jesus (Matthew 5), the fruit of the Spirit (Galatians 5:22-23), Paul's great chapter on love (I Corinthians 13), and Peter's list of characteristics of an effective and productive life (II Peter 1:5-8).

---

43 Genesis 3:5.
44 Ephesians 4:22-24.

When you forget that character is one of God's purposes for your life, you will become frustrated by your circumstances. You may wonder: "Why is this happening to me? Why am I having such a difficult time?" One answer is that life is supposed to be difficult. It's what enables you to grow. Many Christians misinterpret Jesus's promise of an abundant life[45] to mean perfect health, a comfortable lifestyle, constant happiness, full realization of your dreams, and instant relief from problems through faith and prayer. They expect the Christian life to be is easy. They expect heaven on earth.

This self-absorbed perspective treats God as a genie who simply exists to serve you in your selfish pursuit of personal fulfillment. God is not your servant. If you fall for the idea that life is supposed to be easy, you either become severely disillusioned or live in denial of reality.

Never forget that life is not about you. You exist for God's purposes, not vice versa. Why would God provide heaven on Earth when he's planned the real thing for you in eternity? Spend your time on earth preparing for heaven by building your Christlike character.

Did you know that the American Bible Society recently released a report showing that only 9% of Americans read their Bible every day? This is the lowest figure they have reported in over a decade. But here's the good news—67.8% of American adults (about 72 million) are considered Bible-curious, which means they are hungry to learn more about scripture.

Here's some even better news. The data also showed that more Americans were exploring the Bible for the first time after the pandemic hit than ever before. This means there are

---

[45] John 10:10.

literally millions of Americans who are hungry for the Word in addition to those in the rest of the world.

How to Satisfy Your Spiritual Thirst

Do you feel unsatisfied with your life? Are you ready to live a fulfilled, meaningful life? It's time to start looking for satisfaction in Jesus alone. If you're like most people, you're always looking around trying to find something to make your life happy and significant. You think, *If I could just wear these kind of clothes, then I'd be cool. If I could just have plastic surgery and get this fixed, then life would be grand. If I could just get this job, I'd be satisfied.* The pursuit of these things leaves you exhausted because these things will never really satisfy you.

The Bible says: "For my people have done two evil things: they have abandoned me—the fountain of living water. And they have dug for themselves cracked cisterns that can hold no water at all."[46]

Not only have you rejected God and not looked to Him to meet all your needs and satisfy your life, you're also trying to meet your needs on your own. The wells you dug that you call a career, good looks, or the perfect house aren't going to hold water.

In John 4:13-14, Jesus says: "Anyone who drinks this water will soon become thirsty again. But those who drink the water I give will never be thirsty again. It becomes a fresh, bubbling spring within them, giving them eternal life."

Sin is addictive. It only makes you thirstier. If you don't believe that, ask anybody who's looked at pornography— once is not enough. If you are addicted to prescription medication, one pill is never enough. If you have a problem

---

[46] Jeremiah 2:13.

with anger, you're not going to lash out just once. A sin creates greater thirst for satisfaction. That's how it is with every pursuit outside of Jesus. It will only leave you thirstier than you were before.

But Jesus offers living water that will permanently satisfy your thirst. If you feel unsatisfied with your life, you're spiritually thirsty. And the only one who can quench that thirst is Jesus.

What's Your Final Authority?

One fundamental question in life stands above all others: What will have the final authority in your life? Will it be your parents? Your peers? Maybe your friends or your career? Perhaps the books you read? The Bible? The people you follow on social media? What about the movies or shows you watch or the songs you listen to?

All of these sources will shape your values if you let them. It's your values that ultimately determine what has final authority in your life. So what will it be for you?

God allows you to decide. He's given you free will. Most of your authority options fall into these three categories:

1. *Your opinions.* You can depend on your gut to tell you what to do, but there's a problem with that. Studies show your perceptions are more likely to be wrong than right. In fact, sometimes you even lie to yourself. The Bible says the human mind is the most deceitful of all things. It is incurable. No one can understand how deceitful it is.[47]

2. *The world.* You can depend on what other people think to determine your values. However, people

---

[47] Jeremiah 17:9.

often value the wrong things. For instance, the world emphasizes beauty over character, tells you to pursue whatever feels good, and declares that whoever has the most possessions wins. You're bombarded with these worldly values through all sorts of media—so much so that it's easy to start thinking God put you on this planet to look good, feel good, and accumulate stuff. But that couldn't be further from the truth.

3. *God's word.* God's word is objective and truthful, unlike your own perceptions of the world's opinions. God's word says: "If you continue in my word ... you will know the truth and the truth will set you free."[48]

The choice is clear. There's only one authority that's always reliable and will never lead you astray. Decide today to allow God's word to shape your values. Give it the final authority of your life.

My hope for those who have already experienced every negative emotion and loss of hope for a bright future due to crushing consequences and insane restrictions as a result of the COVID pandemic, is that they will finally humble themselves and acknowledge Jesus Christ as the *only trusted source of hope* for every area of life, regardless of circumstances.

Promises of God's Word Compared to Erroneous World Thinking

This section contains various Old and New Testament scriptures found throughout the Bible about God, describing himself as creator, savior, and counselor, along with the desire for how we respond to this plan for our lives. I

---

48 John 8:31-32, *ISV.*

encourage you to match your thinking up against God's clear promises about his love for you as his creation and his playbook for how to respond to his commands and invitations, not only for this brief life, but also for all of eternity... *not peace, but division.*

In an attempt to get your undivided attention about the polar opposites of what God says is truth compared to what the world promotes as truth, I begin with Jesus's words regarding the world's assertion that he came to this Earth to bring peace and unity between the human race. To the contrary, in Luke 12:49-53, Jesus said: "I have come to set the world on fire, and I wish it were already burning! I have a terrible baptism of suffering ahead of me, and I am under a heavy burden until it is accomplished. Do you think I have come to bring peace to the earth? No, I have come to divide people against each other! From now on families will be split apart, three in favor of me, and two against—or two in favor and three against. Father will be divided against son and son against father; mother against daughter and daughter against mother; and mother-in-law against daughter-in-law and daughter-in-law against mother-in-law."

Not even our most distrusted politicians or news reporters from the media could successfully spin this absolute truth from Jesus. Yet year after year they repeat the lie that Jesus is a God of peace, that wants unity or undivided agreement on every position or law they deem appropriate or in line with their twisted thinking—including the killing of unborn babies by the millions.

Look at God's position on the unborn as written in Psalm 139:13-16: "You made all the delicate, inner parts of my body and knit me together in my mother's womb. Thank you for making me so wonderfully complex! Your workmanship is marvelous—how well I know it. You watched me as I was being formed in utter seclusion, as I was woven together in the dark of the womb. You saw me before I was born. Every day of my life was recorded in your book. Every moment was laid out before a single day had passed."

In other words, there are no surprises with God—not car accidents, cancer, or COVID. What this also means is that *no one* will live one day longer or die one day sooner than what God planned for each of us before we were born.

God is Love Whether We Acknowledge Him as Creator of the Universe or Not

Check out God's position and harsh language found in Romans 1:18-22 for those sinful, wicked people he calls utter fools who suppress the truth: "But God shows his anger from heaven against all sinful, wicked people who suppress the truth by their wickedness. They know the truth about God because he has made it obvious to them. For ever since the world was created, people have seen the earth and sky. Through everything God made, they can clearly see his invisible qualities—his eternal power and divine nature. So they have no excuse for not knowing God. Yes, they knew God, but they wouldn't worship him as God or even give him thanks. And they began to think up foolish ideas of what God was like. As a result, their minds became dark and confused. Claiming to be wise, they instead became utter fools."

Also note the conditions found in Psalm 145:17-20 for God's love and provisions for those who love him versus his plan to destroy all who are wicked: "The Lord is righteous in everything he does; he is filled with kindness. The Lord is close to all who call on him, yes, to all who call on him in truth. He grants the desires of those who fear him; he hears their cries for help and rescues them. The Lord protects all those who love him, but he destroys the wicked."

God's Glory, Love, Sovereignty, Provisions, Compassion, and Warnings

"God is our refuge and strength, always ready to help in times of trouble. O we will not fear when earthquakes come and the mountains crumble into the sea." (Psalm 46:1-2)

"Be still and know that I am God. I will be honored by every nation. I will be honored throughout the world." (Psalm 46:10)

"Therefore, God elevated him to the place of highest honor and gave him the name above all other names, that at the name of Jesus every knee should bow, in heaven and on earth and under the earth, and every tongue declare that Jesus Christ is Lord, to the glory of God the Father." (Philippians 2:9-11)

"Study this book of instruction continually. Meditate on it day and night so you will be sure to obey everything written in it. Only then will you prosper and succeed in all you do." (Joshua 1:8)

"For the Lord has comforted his people and will have compassion on them in their suffering." (Isaiah 49:13)

"Seek the Kingdom of God above all else, and live righteously, and he will give you everything you need. So don't worry about tomorrow, for tomorrow will bring its own worries. Today's trouble is enough for today." (Matthew 6:33-34)

"And what do you benefit if you gain the whole world but lose your own soul?" (Mark 8:36)

"The thief's purpose is to steal and kill and destroy. My purpose is to give them a rich and satisfying life." (John 10:10)

"I am the vine; you are the branches. Those who remain in me, and I in them, will produce much fruit. For apart from me you can do nothing." (John 15:5)

"For I can do everything through Christ, who gives me strength." (Philippians 4:13)

"For our present troubles are small and won't last very long. Yet they produce for us a glory that vastly outweighs them and will last forever!" (II Corinthians 4:17)

"Think about what I am saying. The Lord will help you understand all these things." (II Timothy 2:7, 3:17)

"You must have the same attitude that Jesus Christ had." (Philippians 2:5)

"So let it grow, for when your endurance is fully developed, you will be perfect and complete, needing nothing." (James 1:4)

"But don't just listen to God's word. You must do what it says. Otherwise, you are only fooling yourselves." (James 1:22)

Boasting About Tomorrow

"Look here, you who say, 'Today or tomorrow we are going to a certain town and will stay there a year. We will do business there and make a profit.' How do you know what your life will be like tomorrow? Your life is like the morning fog—it's here a little while, then it's gone. What you ought to say is, 'If the Lord wants us to, we will live and do this or that'."[49]

For those who are spiritually blind or indifferent, I pray the previous scriptures convince you to choose Christ and his

---

[49] James 4:13-15.

plan of salvation over your rejection of his love. The following is the plan of salvation to begin a new life:

Step One. Recognize that God loves you and has a plan for your life.

- His love includes you.

  o "For this is how God loved the world: He gave his one and only Son, so that everyone who believes in him will not perish but have eternal life."[50]

- He has a new life for you.

  o "I have come that they may have life and have it to the full."[51]

Step Two: Recognize that sin separates you from God and from others. Sin is walking our own way in rebellion against God's will. When we walk away from God, we walk away from life.

- Everyone has sinned.

  o "For everyone has sinned; we all fall short of God's glorious standard."[52]

- Sin brings death.

  o "For the wages of sin is death."[53]

Step Three: Recognize that Jesus Christ died and rose again for our sins.

- He died in our place.

---

[50] John 3:16.
[51] John 10:10.
[52] Romans 3:23.
[53] Romans 6:23.

- o "But God showed his great love for us by sending Christ to die for us while we were still sinners."54

- Jesus Christ is the way to new life.

  - o "This means that anyone who belongs to Christ has become a new person. The old life is gone; a new life has begun!"55

Step Four: You must repent and ask God for forgiveness.

- Admit and confess your sins to God.

  - o "People who conceal their sins will not prosper, but if they confess and turn from them, they will receive mercy."56

Step Five: Place your trust in Christ and receive him as your savior.

- Christ is ready.

  - o "Look! I stand at the door and knock. If you hear my voice and open the door, I will come in, and we will share a meal together as friends."57

- Receive him now.

  - o "But to all who believed him and accepted him, he gave the right to become children of God."58

Prayer

Father, I believe that Jesus is the way, the truth, and the life and that no one comes to you any other way. Every other

54 Romans 5:8.
55 II Corinthians 5:17.
56 Proverbs 28:13.
57 Revelations 3:20.
58 John 1:12.

way is the wrong way and leads to death. I understand that through your Son's death on the cross, he paid the price for my sins and bridged the gap to eternal life. I know that your way leads to life. Help me to follow where you lead me. I desire to walk in your ways.

Lord Jesus, I want to have life. I know that I have sinned. I need your forgiveness and pardon. I believe that you died and rose again for my sins. I now accept you as my personal Savior. I will forsake my sinful life. I know that your grace and power will enable me to live for you. Thank you, Jesus, for saving me and for giving me a new life. Amen.

Comments from Your Life Coach

Throughout our journey, I have been careful not to "tell you" to do anything, but rather to help you seriously look in the mirror of your Balance Wheel and to discover what is holding you back from living a healthy, fulfilling, peaceful, productive, and balanced life. However, I would have deep regrets if I did not tell you that your number one lifetime decision has to do with your response to the plan of salvation. The truth is that the other 99% of this book's content means *absolutely zero* if you fail to choose your new life in Christ—based on the great sacrifice he paid for you— and continue to choose yourself to be at the center of all your life areas.

I'll remind you again that the mortality rate is 100% and you are going to die someday and face an eternity of trillions upon trillions of years, either in the perfect presence of God in heaven—where no more striving, tears and suffering exist—or in a place God calls hell, where you are separated from everything that is good and experience only grief and pain.

Your greatest choice is to select which you will experience eternally. My sincere hope and prayer is that you will choose a future that you'll never regret.

Knowing God or Knowing About God

"O righteous Father, the world doesn't know you, but I do; and these disciples know you sent me." (John 17:25)

There is a vast difference between knowing God and simply knowing about God. The only way we can get to know God is by spending time in prayer, by reading and studying the scriptures, and by living in obedience to God's word. It is not a one-time experience. It takes patience, perseverance, and endurance. It takes doing it day after day, week after week, month after month, and year after year. It takes a lot of self-discipline. It takes reading God's word more than you read your secular magazines or social media.

Is your relationship with God genuine? Do you love to read God's word? Do you love being around God's people? Do you love to share what God is doing in your life? Is your life bearing the fruits of the spirit? If you really know God rather than simply knowing about God, you should be able to answer these questions affirmatively. Here are five concepts to remember about God and your relationship with him:

- Nothing can set your heart at rest but a real acquaintance with God.

- You will know you are finding God when you believe he is good, no matter what happens.

- Whenever you place a higher priority on solving your problems than on pursuing God, you are immoral and imbalanced.

- Your primary purpose should not be to use God to solve your problems, but to move through your problems toward finding God.

- You find God to the degree that you want to find him.

Admit—Commit—Submit

- What worldview thinking are you ready to *admit* to that is negatively impacting your spiritual decision to accept God's plan for you?

- What biblical view are you ready to *commit* to pursuing to create a new life plan with Christ at the center of your Balance Wheel?

- Who are you prepared to *submit* to for accountability, encouragement, and wisdom to grow and live out your new life plan?

God's Design for Relationship, Not Religion

I designed you to live in union with me. This union does not negate who you are, it actually makes you more fully yourself. When you try to live independently of me, you experience emptiness and dissatisfaction. You may gain the whole world and yet lose everything that really counts. Find fulfillment through living close to me, yielding to my purpose for you. Though, I may lead you along paths that feel alien to you, trust that I know what I am doing. If you follow me wholeheartedly, you will discover facets of yourself that were previously hidden. I know you intimately, far better than you know yourself. In union with me you are complete. In closeness to me, you are transformed more and more into the one I designed you to be.[59]

The most effective way to resist evil is to draw near me. When you need to take action, I will guide you clearly through my spirit and my word. The world is so complex and overstimulating that you can easily lose your sense of direction. Doing the countless unnecessary activities will dissipate your energy. When you spend time with me, I restore your sense of direction. As you look to me for guidance, I enable you to do less, but accomplish more.[60]

This is the ultimate way to slow down in order to speed up!

---

59 Drawn from Mark 8:36; Psalm 139:13-16; II Corinthians 3:17-18. https://www.midlandscbd.com/articles/jesus-calling-september-16-17271.

60 Drawn from Luke 12:20-25; Ephesians 6:12; Proverbs 16:3. https://www.midlandscbd.com/articles/jesus-calling-august-29-16909

12 | Setting Goals for Your Life Development Plan

This chapter lays out a specific and proven plan of action that helps you identify personal life goals and determine what is needed to achieve those goals.

This plan will enable you to distinguish between a life goal and a tangible or numerical goal. The plan will also explain the significance of life goals in establishing a pattern of future success. We will also discuss the importance of including family members and other personal mentors in shaping your life goals by identifying your current goals and prioritizing those for your future.

In order to accomplish these goals, you need to understand:

- You need to have goals for all aspects of your life.

- These personal goals affect one another.

- Family members have a stake in your goals.

- You must set priorities and stay focused on long-term goals.

You'll know you've got it when you can:

- List long and short-term goals in all eight life goal areas

- List the person(s) involved in achieving these goals

Goals should be:

- Written on paper or computer, not in your head

- Short-term, meaning less than a year

- Long-term, a year or more out

- Personal, what you want

- Professional career or business goals needed to attain the personal goals

Reasons why people don't set goals:

- Takes too much time and effort

- Threatening

- Fear of failure

- Don't know how to begin the process

Sandler Rule: "You can't accomplish anything great by playing it safe."

Balance Wheel Goals

You should have goals in all eight areas of your life. Create your individualized process to achieve those personal goals.

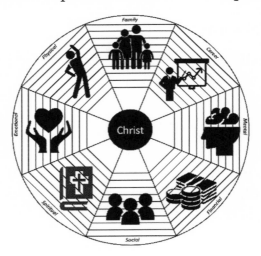

Overview of Goals

Goals are significant because they:

- Force you to define your value system
- Force you to self-set priorities
- Identify a track for you to follow
- Help you manage your behavior
- Help you identify strengths and weaknesses
- Improve self-esteem
- Help you focus your energy
- Motivate you
- Make you stretch

Establish Daily Priorities

Happiness is feeling good about yourself, period. That depends very much on your productivity. Your productivity depends on your ability to set up a list of daily tasks and accomplish them in order of importance.

Make a to-do list each morning of the people you need to call or see, and the things you must do. Write them down and do them in priority order.

Good goals should be SMART—Specific, Measurable, Attainable, Realistic, and Time-bound.

Tangible goals include things like purchasing a new house, fundraising for charitable goals, losing or maintaining weight, earning a college degree, attaining a specific income, or gaining membership to a club.

Intangible goals include things like solidifying your relationship with God, improving relationships with family members, earning the respect of colleagues and the community, and reducing stress.

To conclude this process, your goals need to be based on core values that are set in stone... things like security (having a secure and stable job), service (contributing to the satisfaction of others), friendship (working with people you like and being liked by them in return), challenges and self-realization (work that is personally challenging and helps you grow), family (making a more harmonious life for all members), independence (having freedom of thought, time and action), achievement (accomplishing important things), enjoyment (liking your work and having fun at it), location (living where you want to live), expertise (becoming an authority), prestige (being seen as successful, as having stature), loyalty (being loyal to your company and boss, and having their loyalty in return), wealth (earning lots of money), and leadership (becoming influential).

Now, this is just a list of potential core values. There are others you should choose. But again, remember these should be core, right to the center of you. They are based on what is non-negotiable, whether anyone is looking at you or not. You will live by and be directed by these core values.

Goal-setting Process

Now that you have decided what your future life can look like, use the following steps to set goals.

1. Get eight pieces of paper, or create a file on your personal computer or other electronic device.

   - Label each page for one of the eight life goal areas.

   - Take inventory of where you are right now. Write a brief summary of your present status.

   - Try to work on one goal at a time, to list everything you would like to accomplish now and in the future. Do this for each of the eight life goal areas.

   - Don't prejudge your thoughts. Just write them all down. Include tangible and intangible goals.

2. Prioritize the goals in each of the eight areas from most important to least important.

3. Create a master list of the top three goals from each of the eight areas.

4. Prioritize the master list.

   - Check for balance and any possible conflicts.

   - Make sure the goals aren't too heavily weighted in one or two areas. For example, don't let work goals overshadow family and health goals.

5. Write a detailed description of each goal and how you are going to achieve it. Remember, the goals must be SMART—specific, measurable, attainable, realistic, and time-bound.

- The goals should make you stretch. It's okay to fantasize a little. If some of your goals aren't a bit crazy, then they are probably too realistic.

- Include what you can do right now as well as what you want to be able to do in the future.

6. Decide on a timetable for each goal. Break down the long-term goals into short-term activities with deadlines.

   - Be sure to include monthly, weekly, and daily activities.

7. Share your goals with others, especially those who are affected by the goals, such as family, friends, and colleagues.

8. Review your goals regularly and track your progress.

9. Be persistent.

   - Your priorities will change over time. You might need to redefine or realign your goals.

   - Abandon a goal only if it becomes irrelevant, not because it's too hard.

Wrap-up

In this part of your journey, you have learned the importance of establishing written goals in all areas of your life: spiritual, physical, social, financial, mental, educational, work, family, and personal. You have seen that both tangible and intangible goals are important. And you realize that it is your intangible goals that continue to drive you to new heights on a tangible level.

The time between now and your planned retirement is the time you have available to work consistently on those goals, particularly the ones which require business and professional activity in order to be accomplished. Your personal goals and your business goals are related in this fashion.

It is extremely important not only to write your goals, but also to prioritize them so that focus and momentum can be maintained. Each goal requires a plan of attack and a timetable—in other words, a way to accomplish it in its time.

Goals should be shared with significant others so that they become a part of your life together rather than yours alone. Finally, and most importantly, determine that you are willing to do whatever it takes for however long it takes to reach your goals. If your response isn't a resounding yes, consider the possibility that the goal doesn't actually deserve to be included.

If someone were to ask you exactly what you have pictured for yourself one year from now, two years from now, or five years from now, how clear would those pictures be? Goal setting gives you a track to run on. Goal setting forces you to establish priorities. Goal setting separates reality from wishful thinking. Goal setting makes you responsible for your own life. It forces you to define and establish your own value system. Your commitment to this process will determine what your future life can be. This is your moment to decide your future!

13 | HOW TO CHOOSE
WHAT IS IMPORTANT VS. URGENT

Now that we have broken down each area of your Balance Wheel and given you a proven, repeatable plan to change and achieve those life goals, I will expose you to more incredible tools to help you make the tough decisions, to move from a life of urgency—which is filled with managing one crisis after another—to a life of importance, based on things that really matter most.

Goethe said, "Things that matter most should never be at the mercy of things that matter least." In other words, how do we achieve the Return On Energy (ROE) we have been discussing as a result of changed thinking, which leads to changed behaviors on the way to a balanced and fulfilling life?

How do we move from a life of crisis management to a life of living by our core values, determining what's really important to us? We've talked about the timing of change; it's never too late to change! Remember, the goal is not necessarily change, but rather improvement. So that's why we look at the Imbalance Wheel to help us identify our blind spots, to do a gap analysis on our current life so we can determine why we are exhausted and fed up with not having a balanced life.

Now we're aware of what's creating that. We're aware of the specific reasons for the inconsistencies between what we say we want versus what we're actually doing to achieve what we want. That being said, this chapter will lean on sources, concepts, and principles that I have been exposed to for the past 50 years of studying leadership and management, to really understand the difference between leading your life versus managing your existence.

But for today's conversation, this chapter is designed to help you understand how to manage your life because you cannot manage time. *Time management* is a misnomer. If you want to make an impact with your life, you've got to do one thing— get control of your time. Your time is your life. If you don't learn to control your time, you limit the legacy of your life. The Bible says: "Be careful how you live. Don't live like fools, but like those who are wise. Make the most of every opportunity in these evil days. Don't act thoughtlessly, but understand what the Lord wants you to do."[61]

We all have the same amount of time every week... 168 hours. It's what you do with it that counts. You've only been allotted a certain number of days in this world, and if you waste them, you've blown it. If you waste time, you're wasting your life because your time is your life. You have to stop and ask, "Is this the best use of my time? Is this the best use of my life?" You don't have time for everything.

The good news is that God doesn't expect you to do everything, so don't feel guilty about it. There are only a few things worth doing in the first place, which we will be talking about when we cover "first things first." Matthew 6:33 says: "Seek the Kingdom of God above all else, and live righteously, and he will give you everything you need."

Effective people figure out what's essential in life and what's trivial, and they spend more time doing the essential things

---

[61] Ephesians 5:15-17.

and less time doing the trivial things. You can't eliminate all the trivia in your life, but you can reduce it.

This sounds easy, but frankly, it's often difficult to choose between what's best for your life and what's easiest, especially when you're tired. When you're tired, you don't want to do the best thing; you want to do what's easy. That's why if you're really going to make something of your life, you have to learn to get some rest. If you're not rested, you won't have the mental, emotional, and physical strength to say, "I'm going to do the right thing instead of the easiest thing."

In each day, everyone has 24 hours. No one has more. No one has less. The 10% achieve much greater success and balance because they focus on what they can control—their behaviors, because they've identified what those specific important behaviors are in each area of their lives. So whether it's our spiritual, mental, physical, emotional, financial, work, career, social, or family areas of our lives, we have determined that lack of time is not the problem, but the realization that the behaviors we are doing or not doing are producing a life of imbalance filled with so much needless stress and failure.

To help us move forward to living a fulfilled and balanced life, remember the concepts and core principles contained in Stephen Covey's *Seven Habits of Highly Effective People.*

I have used these concepts in my career as a Sandler Training coach and facilitator of growth to complement the revolutionary work of David H. Sandler when he wrote his bestselling book, *You Can't Teach a Kid to Ride a Bike at a Seminar.* This encompassed all his human dynamics, psychology and training courses impacting sales and sales management he created back in the 1970s, '80s and '90s, Sandler's entire life's work was built around the concept of what we call Inside/Outside change, emphasizing that until you can see yourself differently and accept your identity as a one of a kind, valuable human being, you cannot behave differently—meaning your extrinsic value as a Human Doing did not determine your intrinsic value as a Human Being. This is the polar opposite of what the world pressures you to believe.

Covey's *Seven Habits* are based on a similar theory. Habits 1, 2, and 3 represent one's private or inside victory, which is foundational to Habits 4, 5, and 6, which represent one's public victory or outside victory. The bottom line is that until you see yourself differently and you have goals to create something different, you are not going to achieve sustainable change in growth and improvement in your life.

In this section we will focus on Covey's third habit where he talks about "First Things First"—the habit of the private victory.

Covey explains that it begins with organizing and executing around your priorities. We've already spent a lot of time talking about how the 10% execute around their priorities. Now let's see how you can determine and organize your priorities.

What Priorities Drive My Focus

I Immediate	II Significant
- Big Trouble - Incidents - Hot Potato - Emergency - Catastrophe	- Essential - Meaningful - Highly Relevant - Substantial - Exceptional
- Repetitive Activities - Non-essential - Uncertainties - Contingencies - Predicaments	- Insignificant - Frivolous - Meaningless - Trivial - Unnecessary
III Secondary	IV Insignificant

Figure 12-1

The four quadrants show you truly what crisis management is. Quadrant I describes a life of crisis based on an unhealthy sense of urgency. A few of the critical Quadrant I indicators are:

- Crises
- Pressing Problems
- Fire Fighting
- Major Scrap or Rework
- Deadline-driven projects

Yes, at the time of their occurrence, these issues or situations are important, but people who spend most of their waking hours in this quadrant seem to be addicted by the sense of urgency. So they regularly move from one crisis to another, leaving very little margin in their lives for anyone or anything of real importance. Typically, you'll find the high drivers and the Type-A personalities and the perfectionists operating in this quadrant, rationalizing that they are the ones who get things done.

Now, we want to look at Quadrant II where the focus is not on the urgent, but rather what is important, where all things you decide that used to be crises—that used to be pleasurable, that used to be of necessity, that used to be proximate and pressing things to do—can be moved to the Quadrant II of importance.

Based on doing the effective activities of prevention, production capability, relationship building, recognizing new opportunities, and planning, when you make the decision to focus on Quadrant II, the search to save hours a day will occur in Quadrants III and IV by scrutinizing the activities so many people currently waste so much of their time and energy on—"Doing the Things that Matter Least."

Remember that the goal is ultimately to determine which activities are really important based on the life goals we discussed in the last chapter. This is where you must decide to stop doing minor activities in order to achieve major life improvements and balance.

Quadrant III activities fall in the urgent but not important category and include:

- Interruptions
- Some calls, email, and reports
- Some meetings
- Proximate pressing matters
- Popular activities

Lastly, the real time savings come from your Quadrant IV evaluation of activities that are neither urgent nor important, which include:

- Trivial items

- Busywork
- Most email, text, and phone calls
- Time wasters
- Pleasant activities

Note: Social Media as a Whole...

Research has recently revealed that the average amount of time online and social media is now 7-11 hours per day for many people, either being on it or thinking they need to be on it... like you would actually miss anything of importance. Prior to that, we talked about TV consuming 5-7 hours a day as the national average, but not for the 10-percenters living balanced lives! Changing your TV and social media habits, and avoiding time-wasting activities is where you'll be able to regain countless hours each day.

*A day that is a social media success
is usually a business and life failure.*

But even more importantly, you will greatly eliminate the drain on your energy and emotional well-being of being pulled in all the different directions by either signals, or vibrations, or actual rings and dings in your pocket or purse, allowing you to experience a quieter existence and a more soothing experience in life. As a result, you will develop the ability to say "Yes" to what's important and "No" to everything else.

*Note: At the time of writing, a whistleblower from Facebook is appearing before the U.S. Congress and Senate, providing evidence that Facebook CEO Mark Zuckerberg was aware for more than ten years that nearly a third of young girls on the platform were drastically harmed by Facebook encounters, leading to cases of depression and suicide.

To become a world-class, effective human being, remember to shift from temporal to eternal thinking. This will help you stop focusing on minor issues and distinguish between what's urgent and important. So much of what we waste our energy on will not matter even a year from now, much less for all eternity.[62]

We are going to be dead a lot longer than we are going to be alive. So we should get over whatever is holding us back so we can get on with it!

Closing Challenge

Don't waste your life. Don't settle for second best. Don't go through life just existing. You were not created to just coast. God made you for a mission and a purpose. That starts by asking yourself: "Is what I'm doing the best use of my life?"

- What things take most of your time?

- How much are those things helping you fulfill your mission in life?

- What can you change in your schedule and priorities so that you can get more rest?

Colossians 3:17 says: "Whatever you do or say, do it as a representative of the Lord Jesus, giving thanks through him to God the Father."

---

[62] Drawn from Rick Warren's *Purpose Driven Life.*

14 | CONCLUSION

Burning the bridge to your Imbalance Wheel

---

*"Forgetting the past and looking forward
to what lies ahead, I press on to reach the
end of the race and receive the heavenly
prize for which God, through Christ Jesus,
is calling us." (Philippians 3:13-14)*

Yes, everyone has giants which appear to stand between our dreams and our current reality. So this journey has been about helping you discover the common denominator that holds the 90% back from achieving a life of peace, fulfillment, and balance. That answer has been, currently is, and will always be the choice of *who* you place at the center of your Balance Wheel—yourself or Jesus Christ.

The reality is that we are all products of our past, but need not remain as prisoners of it. It is time for you to choose to burn the bridges to your self-imposed prison of living a life of imbalance.

Review Time—Reset and Restart!

Who is in control of your life's Balance Wheel?

Use the Balance Triangle to determine how your attitudes, behaviors, skills, core values, and beliefs are affected by worldview versus biblical view. Your character development and personal habits lead either to a life of balance or imbalance.

Use the Hedgehog concept of BHAG (big, hairy, audacious goals) to determine what you are deeply passionate about, what you will decide to be best-in-the-world at, and what will drive your economic engine.

Consider how you want to spend the rest of your life to add urgency and awareness of your ability to change and improve your life. Awareness of ineffective or unproductive attitudes, behaviors, and skills—as well as new and improved attitudes, behaviors, and skills—will help you live like a 10-percenter who achieves a higher degree of life balance.

The choice is yours and yours alone to opt for change and improvement over insanity. Winners adjust their thinking and behave themselves into a good attitude versus waiting to feel good before taking responsibility and doing what they don't necessarily feel like doing.

Use the AKASH model to further your change and improve decisions:

- Awareness
- Knowledge
- Application
- Skills development
- Habit formation

Set goals for each of the eight areas of the Balance Wheel. Remember to prioritize what is important versus urgent.

Throughout our journey, you have been confronted with the insanity of believing that your best thinking, which has resulted in so many hurtful and unfulfilling outcomes, will somehow produce better outcomes in the future. I remind you that you cannot wish yourself out of something you behaved yourself into. So our closing part of our journey together will challenge you to choose all the future God has for you, by reminding you of his love and plans for you, along with resources available to everyone to trust the *ultimate dream giver*.

As your temporary life coach, I pray you are prepared to leave your current reality of being "ordinary," living in the land of the familiar (mediocre comfort zones) with your head trash, failures, bitterness, and regrets, and move toward your Land of Promise as a "Somebody" who is willing to face the giants holding you back.

For those who are ready, the process outlined in this chapter will guide you to move from mediocre to good, good to great, and great to significant and finally *admit* that your thoughts, words, actions, and habits are the reasons for your life of imbalance. Once you take 100% responsibility for your life with no excuses, you will be able to *commit* to a new way of living your life with purpose, and *submit* to God who is able to provide you with the direction and strength in order to achieve and thrive as you fulfill your dreams and life purpose.

What Drives Your Life

There are five great benefits of living a purpose-driven life:

- Knowing your purpose gives your life meaning.
- Knowing your purpose simplifies your life.
- Knowing your purpose focuses your life.
- Knowing your purpose motivates your life.
- Fulfilling your purpose will create an eternal legacy.

Everyone wants to be remembered when they're gone. Ultimately, what matters most will not be what others say about your life, but what God says about you. How will you answer God when asked, "What did you do with what I gave you?"

Since thinking differently has been the second-most important emphasis throughout *Life of Balance*, let's consider Steve Seibold's *Secrets of the World Class: Turning Mediocrity into Greatness* as we compare how the 90% consider life compared to those in the 10% of high achievement and life balance.

World-class vs. Middle-class Thinking

- The middle-class *compete...*
  The world-class *create.*

- The middle-class *avoid risk...*
  The world-class *manage risk.*

- The middle-class love to be *comfortable...*
  The world-class are *comfortable being uncomfortable.*

- The middle-class live in *delusion...*
  The world-class live in *objective reality.*

- The middle-class hunger for *security...*
  The world-class understand that *security does not exist.*

God Made You to Be You

God planned every single day of your life. Before you took your first breath, God knew everything that would ever happen to you. Long before you were conceived by your biological parents, you were conceived in the mind of God. It is not by fate, chance, luck, or coincidence that you are breathing at this very moment.

You're alive right now because God wants you to be—with all your strengths and weaknesses. Whether your parents were good, bad, or indifferent, God used them. They had the exact DNA needed to create you. From the beginning of time, God had a plan for your life and a purpose he wants you to complete. God made you to be you.

You were not just another baby born. God personally planned for your birth. You are God's masterpiece. He made you so he could love you and so you could fulfill his purposes in this world. At different seasons of life, you may struggle to see what that purpose is, but you never have to doubt that it's there. Before you were born, God gave you a purpose.

Even Your Weaknesses Bring Glory to God

Spiritual gifts, heart, abilities, personality, and experiences— these are the five things that make you you. Accepting your "SHAPE"—the unique way God made you to bring glory to him—means to believe God knows best. It all comes down to a matter of trust. Do you believe God made a mistake when he made you? Or do you trust him knowing he has a plan for your life?

Many of us make these kinds of statements to God: "There are things I don't like about myself. I wish I had a different hair color. I wish I were taller, shorter, skinnier. I wish I had more talent. I wish I could do that. I wish I looked like him. I wish I had her smarts..." and on and on. This kind of thinking is basically telling God, "You blew it. Everybody else is OK, but you goofed up when you made me." When you reject yourself, you are in essence rejecting God because he's your creator.

When you don't accept yourself, it's rebellion against God. You're saying, "God, I know better than you. You should have made me differently with a different set of strengths and a different set of weaknesses." But God says, "No, I created you exactly the way you are because I want you to be you with your strengths and your weaknesses. All that can give me glory—if you'll just start doing what I made you to do instead of trying to be like everybody else."

It's actually quite arrogant to reject yourself. Romans 9:20 says: "Who are you, a mere human being, to argue with God? Should the thing that was created say to the one who created it, 'Why have you made me like this'?"

Whenever you doubt God's love and wisdom, you get yourself into trouble. The root behind many of life's problems is that you don't trust God. You don't believe God really loves you. You don't believe he really has your best interests at heart. You wish he had made you something different. As a result, you foster a spirit of bitterness that produces frustration and keeps you from being the person God wants you to be. But you don't have to live that way. There is hope.

Job 10:10 says: "You guided my conception and formed me in the womb." God wanted you and loves you. He shaped you just the way you are for his glory. Believe it and then trust it!

World-class vs. Middle-class Thinking

- The middle-class focus on *having*...
  The world-class focus on *being*.

- The middle-class have a *lottery mentality*...
  The world-class have an *abundance mentality*.

- The middle-class *slow down*...
  The world-class *calm down*.

- The middle-class are *frustrated*...
  The world-class are *grateful*.

- The middle-class operate out of *fear and scarcity*...
  The world-class operate from *love and abundance*.

- The middle-class has *pipe dreams*...
  The world-class has *vision*.

Settle Your Salvation Today

When the criminal hanging next to Jesus on the cross asked Jesus to remember him, Jesus replied: "I assure you, today you will be with me in paradise."[63] With this response, Jesus gave four characteristics of salvation that you can trust and believe in.

First, he said, today when you die, you either go straight into the presence of God or you go straight into separation from God. Salvation is immediate. The moment you ask Jesus to save you, it's done.

Second, salvation is certain. He said, "Today you will..." He didn't say, "You might" or "I hope..." His answer wasn't, "Let me think about it." Jesus said, "Today you will." When you accept Christ, you can be certain of your salvation.

Third, salvation is a relationship. Jesus said, "You will be with me." Salvation is not a religion. It's not rules or regulations or rituals. It's a relationship. That relationship doesn't begin when you get to heaven. It begins here on Earth. Jesus Christ wants to be your best friend; he wants to talk with you all the time. God made you for a relationship with him!

Fourth, Jesus said, "Today you will be with me in paradise." Heaven is a real place and it's forever.

---

[63] Luke 23:43.

Two criminals were crucified with Jesus, one on either side. Jesus gave them the choice of salvation and he gives you the same choice. He won't force you to love him. He's not going to force you to trust him or to accept heaven.

One of the two criminals rejected Jesus. The other turned to him in faith. You have the same choice. Romans 10:13 says: "Everyone who calls on the name of the Lord will be saved." Do you believe these truths about salvation? Are you ready to call on the name of the Lord?

An Invitation for Now and Eternity

In Greek and Roman mythology, all the gods like Zeus, Jupiter, and Apollo have human frailties. They get angry. They lust. They're impatient. They zap people with lightning bolts. They are inconsistent and unreliable. But the real God—the God who created the universe—is 100% pure and unpolluted. He's never done anything wrong, impure, or imperfect. That's called Holiness.

Habakkuk 1:13 says: "But you are pure and cannot stand the sight of evil." Because God is 100% perfect, you can trust him, unlike the gods of mythology. But his perfection also means that he cannot stand to be around sin. So at the cross, God took every sin of the world and poured it all on his perfect Son, Jesus Christ, who volunteered to do it. It's why he came to Earth!

What Jesus did for you on the cross is called substitution. If Jesus hadn't been your substitute, then you would have to pay for your own sins. God didn't want that, so he sent Jesus to be your substitution. Jesus satisfied the law. He did what justice demanded, but it wasn't easy for Jesus. In fact, it was torture.

You know how bad you feel when you feel guilty over one sin. How would you like to carry the guilt over every horrific act ever done, every sin done against another person, all the sins done in secret? That would be mental, physical, emotional, and spiritual torture on the cross. Jesus cried out: "My God, my God, why have you abandoned me?"[64] He was not just experiencing physical agony. He was experiencing the torment of being separated from his spiritual Father.

A God who is holy could not stand even to look at his son full of all the sins of the world. God looked away because he is perfect. Can you imagine what this cost Jesus? But he was willing to go through that pain because he wanted you to have a way to be in fellowship with a holy God. Somebody had to take the punishment and Jesus did it for you. Jesus became your substitute so that when God looks at you, he won't see your sin. He will see the righteousness of Jesus Christ. And because of that, you can experience both eternal life and a full and purposeful life here on Earth.

Ask yourself:

- Why is it loving for God to be full of justice?

- What does substitution reveal to us about God's character?

- How do you think you should respond to the truth that Jesus suffered and died for you on the cross?

If you haven't trusted in Jesus and committed to following him, why wait any longer?

II Corinthians 6:2 says: "Indeed, the 'right time' is now. Today is the day of salvation." Choose to settle the issue of

---

64 Matthew 27:46.

your eternal destiny today. Trust Jesus's promise of salvation.

You could start by praying this prayer:

> *Dear Jesus, you have promised that if I believe in you, everything I've ever done wrong will be forgiven. I will learn the purpose of my life and you will accept me into your eternal home in heaven one day. Thank you that I can be sure you will fulfill your promise, that I can be assured of my salvation. I confess my sin and I believe you are God, my Savior. I receive you into my life as my Lord. Today I'm turning every part of my life over to you. I want to follow you and do what you tell me to do.*
>
> *Jesus, I am grateful for your love and sacrifice that make it possible for me to join you in heaven. Thank you that I don't have to earn or work for my salvation, because I know that is impossible. I want to use the rest of my life to serve you instead of serving myself. I humbly commit my life to you and I ask you to save me and accept me into your family. In Jesus name, I pray. Amen.*[65]

World-class vs. Middle-class Thinking

- The middle-class *deny their intuition...*
  The world-class *embrace their intuition.*

- The middle-class *trade time for money...*
  The world-class *trade ideas for money.*

---

[65] If you just prayed to accept Jesus, please email Rick Warren at Rick@PastorRick.com and let him know and he will gladly send you some free materials to help you start your journey with Jesus.

- The middle-class are *problem-oriented...*
  The world-class are *solution-oriented.*

- The middle-class see themselves as *victims...*
  The world-class see themselves as *responsible.*

- The middle-class *think they know enough...*
  The world-class are *eager to learn.*

- The middle-class *speak the language of fear...*
  The world-class *speak the language of love.*

Fresh Start—How Will You Respond?

If you Googled the phrase "fresh start," you would get more than two billion results! Evidently a lot of people would like to have a fresh start in life. They think, "I've blown it. I've really made a mess of things in my life. I'd like a fresh start."

Perhaps you are one of those people. You may feel hopeless or helpless. You may think you're unworthy. You may think you're too old or too young. You may think you've done too many bad things. You may think you don't need God, but you do. Or maybe you think God doesn't want you, but he does. You may think you've committed the unpardonable sin, but you haven't. No matter what's happened in your life, God wants a relationship with you. Jesus is in the business of giving people a fresh start.

The apostle Peter said: "Because Jesus was raised from the dead, we've been given a brand new life and have everything to live for, including a future in heaven."[66]

When you give your life to Christ, several things happen:

- You open up your life to God and get to know him.

---

[66] I Peter 1:3-4, *MSG.*

- You're given a brand new life which gives you everything to live for.

- You get a future in heaven.

Rick Warren likes to say it this way: "You get your past forgiven, a purpose for living, and a home in heaven." What a deal! Your past, present, and future are taken care of as you put your trust in Jesus.

Remembering you are not God helps you live in freedom. You don't need to take responsibility for matters that are beyond your control—which includes most matters. If you let go of everything that is not your responsibility, you are freed from carrying unnecessary burdens and you can be more effective in areas where you do have some control. Moreover, you can pray about all your concerns, trusting in God's sovereignty. Bringing him your prayers with Thanksgiving, present your request to him. Living this way will shield you from anxiety and bless you with the peace that passes all understanding.

World-class vs. Middle-class Thinking

- The middle-class choose *fear*...
  The world-class choose *growth*.

- The middle-class are *boastful*...
  The world-class are *humble*

- The middle-class seek *riches*...
  The world-class seek *wealth*.

- The middle-class *believe their vision only when they see it*...
  The world-class *believe in their vision*.

- The middle-class believe problem-solving stems from *knowledge*...
  The world-class believe problem-solving stems from *will*.

- The middle-class coach through *logic*...
  The world-class coach through *emotion*.

Middle-class consciousness is what most of us are born into. World-class consciousness is what's possible. *Failure is never final!* You're never a failure until you quit, and it's always too soon to quit.

You don't determine a person's greatness by their talent, wealth, or education. You determine a person's greatness by what it takes to discourage them. So what does it take to discourage you from going after your dream? It may be as simple as a friend or family member saying, "I don't think that's a good idea."

There are lots of things in your life you don't have control over. You can't control who your parents are, when you were born, or what your race or nationality is. You can't control what gifts and talents you were given, but you do have complete control over how much you choose to believe God.

God uses people who act, who never give up, who take risks in faith, who get God's dream and go after it. It's your choice whether you want to be that kind of person God uses to accomplish his purpose.

Never, Never, Never Give Up

Winners are just ex-losers who got mad at the right person. The battle belongs to the persistent. The victory will go to the one who never quits. Refuse to let circumstances or friends defeat you.

From the ashes of defeat burn the greatest fires of accomplishment. God made you to climb, not crawl. God made you to fly, not fall. God made you to soar, not sink. You were not made to dig in dirt with chickens, but to soar the clouds with the wings of an eagle.

Philippians 4:13 says: "I can do everything through Christ, who gives me strength."

There are three types of people in the world:

- *Accusers*—people who blame everyone else for their problems and shortcomings, constantly accusing other people of causing unhappiness in their lives.

- *Excusers*—people who don't blame others. They just make up excuses for why they don't do more with their lives and their time. Rational lies sound good to them, so they believe those lies. When excusers want to procrastinate, any excuse will do.

- *Choosers*—people who choose responsibility for their lives. They are as happy, as disciplined, and as busy as they want to be. It's their choice.

Which one do you want to be?

Admit—Commit—Submit

- Hopefully you are finally ready to *admit* that you are responsible for your Imbalance Wheel.

- If so, are you ready to *commit* to a new way of living?

- Are you ready to *submit* to Jesus Christ, the Savior of the world, trusting in him for a future that's balanced and fulfilled?

Closing Scripture

"Love the Lord your God with all your heart, all your soul, all your mind, and all your strength." (Mark 12:30)

"Trust in the Lord with all your heart; do not depend on your own understanding. Seek his will in all you do, and he will show you which path to take." (Proverbs 3:5-6)

"'For I know the plans I have for you,' says the Lord. 'They are plans for good and not for disaster, to give you a future and a hope'." (Jeremiah 29:11)

Closing Challenge

"Build a better world," said God. And I answered how the world is such a vast place and so complicated now. And I'm so small and helpless, there's nothing I can do. But God, in all His wisdom said, "Just build a better you. And when you build a better you, you will build better families, better churches, better organizations and a better world."

—Gordon Graham, *Change Is an Inside Job*

How will you answer God?

ACKNOWLEDGMENTS

There are two types of mentors in life: direct mentors like parents, teachers, coaches, leaders, close friends and pastors, who come alongside you on your life journey, and indirect mentors like books containing life stories and examples of wisdom, strength, and courage that provide models of excellence to emulate.

Proverbs 27:17 describes these people: "As iron sharpens iron, so a friend sharpens a friend." These are people God brings into our lives to build up, challenge, encourage, and equip us to become all he designed us to be.

With tremendous gratitude to those who have shaped me and helped me learn these concepts, principles, philosophies, and skills, this section is for you.

First and foremost, I thank God and his word, the Bible, and you for passing them along to me and for the privilege of allowing me to share them with you. Early in life I was specifically influenced by local businessmen, E.B. Frock, Harold Trone, and Dewey James, who have already passed away, but not their kindness and life lessons they gave to me. At age 21, this twelfth-grade-educated kid was given the opportunity to begin a sales and management career in the trucking industry, at a $200 million company owned by Jerry Hall, who saw something in me and provided me with various opportunities to grow. Ten years later I was highly influenced by Will Potter, CEO of a more than $400M company, who later gave me the opportunity at age 35 to develop Preston University as Director of Training for a sales force of 200 and 6,000 company team members. Over the next five years of conducting a multitude of training sessions, these experiences fine-tuned my preparation as a life and business coach, which led Tibby and me to pursue our temporary insanity story at age 39, to begin our now 32-year old business, which allowed me to be greatly impacted by my friends, David Sandler and David Mattson, founders and owners of Sandler Training, allowing me to experience a fulfilling life of sharing those life lessons and practical skill sets with thousands of individuals and organizations.

Special thanks to the talent, expertise, and encouragement of my publisher and dear friend, Demi Stevens. She has allowed me to continue my life's purpose of encouraging others to break the chains of their past and take 100% responsibility for their futures.

With special pride, I thank three of my grandchildren, Morgan, Abby, and Jacob, for their help and talented contributions with content and graphics.

And to Tibby, my lifelong partner and wife of 51 years, eternal thanks for your love, support, and encouragement over the years, to keep fighting the good fight and to finish the race with commitment and passion.

Creating a balanced life does not end with reading a single book. Your response to its contents—creating your individual plan to develop your Balance Triangle, Balance Wheel Core Competencies, and Growth Strategies—will take ongoing, gradual, and incremental effort.

KEEP THE MOMENTUM GOING!

If you are SERIOUS about taking control of the future trajectory of your life, I invite you to call me or visit:

lifeofbalancebook.com
1-888-261-2497

Arrange your complimentary call today regarding coaching and training resources designed to help you on your future personal development journey.

lifeofbalancebook.com
1-888-261-2497

Ed Staub
10 Corral Rd.
Hazleton, Pennsylvania 18202 USA

RESOURCES

Andrews, Andy. *The Butterfly Effect: How Your Life Matters*. Thomas Nelson, 2021.

Andrews, Andy. *The Seven Decisions: Understanding the Keys to Personal Success*. Thomas Nelson, 2014.

Andrews, Andy. *The Traveler's Gift: Seven Decisions that Determine Personal Success*. Thomas Nelson, 2002.

Bradberry, Travis and Jean Greaves. *The Emotional Intelligence Quick Book: Everything You Need to Know to Put Your EQ to Work*. Fireside, 2005.

Britton, Dan and Jimmy Page. *Wisdom Walks: 40 Life Principles for a Significant and Meaningful Journey*. Broadstreet, 2014.

Buford, Bob. *Finishing Well: What People Who Really Live Do Differently*. Integrity, 2004.

Collins, Jim. *Good to Great: Why Some Companies Make the Leap... and Others Don't*. Harper Business, 2001.

Covey, Stephen R. *The 7 Habits of Highly Effective People: Powerful Lessons in Personal Change*. Franklin Covey: 1989.

Johnson, Spencer. *Who Moved My Cheese? An A-Mazing Way to Deal with Change in Your Work and in Your Life*. G.P. Putnam's Sons, 1998.

Mattson, David. *The Road to Excellence: 6 Leadership Strategies to Build a Bulletproof Business*. Sandler Systems, 2018.

Mattson, David & Bruce Seidman. *Sandler Success Principles*. Pegasus Media World, 2012.

Mattson, David. *The Sandler Rules for Sales Leaders*. Sandler Systems, 2017.

Newberry, Tommy. *The 4:8 Principle: The Secret to a Joy-Filled Life*. Tyndale House, 2007.

Rosenberg, Merrick. *The Chameleon: Life-Changing Wisdom for Anyone Who Has a Personality or Knows Someone Who Does*. Take Flight Learning, 2016.

Rosenberg, Merrick, and Daniel Silvert. *Taking Flight! Master the Four Behavioral Styles and Transform Your Career, Your Relationships... Your Life*. FT Press, 2012.

Sandler, David H. *You Can't Teach a Kid to Ride a Bike at a Seminar: Sandler Training's 7-Step System for Successful Selling*. 2nd ed. McGraw Hill, 2015.

Stanley, Thomas J. *The Millionaire Mind*. Andrews McMeel, 2001.

Stoltz, Paul G. *Adversity Quotient: Turning Obstacles into Opportunities*. Wiley, 1999.

The One Year Bible: The entire New Living Translation arranged in 365 daily readings. Tyndale House, 1996.

Warren, Rick. *The Purpose Driven Life: What on Earth Am I Here For?* Zondervan, 2013.

Wilkinson, Bruce. *The Dream Giver*. Multnomah, 2003.

About the Author

ED STAUB serves as owner of Staub & Associates, Franchisee of Sandler Training, an International Sales, Leadership and Human Dynamics Training and Coaching Organization, specializing in providing ongoing, gradual, and incremental learning to people who are serious about their personal and professional development.

Growing up in southcentral Pennsylvania, the third of seven siblings raised by a single mother, Ed decided at a very early age that he intended to break away from the pattern of a drunken and abusive father, and began praying for and visualizing becoming a dedicated husband and father, based on developing life values of love, harmony, and hard work. By God's grace, Ed was influenced in his adolescent years by three different local business owners who took him under their wings.

This ultimately set the groundwork for Ed's 50-year business career, beginning with 20 years as a salesperson, terminal manager, and director of employee training with two of the United States' top 15 trucking companies, which lead to the

32-year creation and development of the Sandler/Staub business he currently shares with his daughters Kate and Kelly, offering a blend of spiritual, mental, and physical principles that promote living a life of balance.

As an author and speaker, Ed is committed to challenging people to transform their lives by walking with Jesus Christ and influencing others.

He is married to his beloved wife Tibby and they reside in their Eagle Rock family home in the northeastern Pennsylvania Pocono Mountains, providing the home base for their clan of 17, entailing three married children and their spouses—Bob and MaryBeth, Kelly and Jeremy, Kate and Calvin—seven grandchildren—Jacob, Morgan, Peyton, Trevor and wife Kenzie, Abby, Alex, and Tyler—and one great grandchild, Brooks.

Made in the USA
Middletown, DE
24 January 2022

58515762R00120